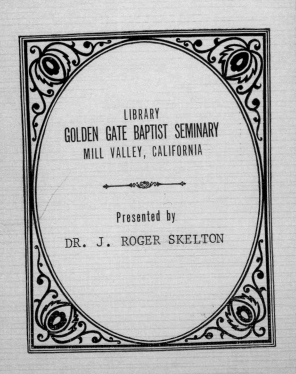

HOW TO GROW A CHURCH

by Donald A. McGavran with Win C. Arn

 A Division of G/L Publications 4863/4
Glendale, California, U.S.A.

Second Printing, 1974
Third Printing, 1975

Second Edition, 1976
Fourth Printing, 1976

Published by
Regal Books Division, G/L Publications
Glendale, California 91209, U.S.A.

Library of Congress Catalog Card No. 73-80207
ISBN 0-8307-0238-5

This book is dedicated to the strengthening of present churches and planting of new churches across America throughout all segments of society. Toward that end we, the co-authors, have labored together and in so doing have found a bond of friendship, common purpose and Christian love.

Contents

Foreword

Donald McGavran believes that the Church today stands poised on the threshold of a new age of explosive growth. Whether or not this new age actually comes about, however, depends on the willingness of Christians to commit themselves to evangelism and follow biblical principles for church growth. I share this conviction.

This is an exciting book, which is at once both simple and profound. The authors challenge us to expect great things when God's work is done in God's way. They point out that one of the greatest enemies to the growth of churches nationwide is complacency. Such complacency, however, not only is contrary to the command of our Lord, but neglects as well the unique opportunities we have before us. Countless millions are unreached with the gospel, and yet many would respond if only Christians would make known the good news of Christ.

Dr. McGavran and Dr. Arn rightly see that the local congregation is the focal point of God's reconciling work in Christ. Evangelism should spring from the church and should always relate new Christians back to the church. Particularly helpful is the insight into practical ways of evaluating the true effectiveness of a church's outreach. Their grasp of the biblical principles of church growth is significant, and their burden for the souls of men and women cannot help but challenge us all to a healthy reexamination and recommitment.

This book could be one of the most significant books of this decade—for the Church. The principles, if applied, would revolutionize the ministry and outreach of thousands of churches and hundreds of thousands of laymen throughout our nation. The first edition of this book has been greatly blessed by God, and I have personally seen the way God has used it in the lives of many congregations. My prayer is that God will use this second edition in an even greater way to touch the hearts of Christians everywhere.

Billy Graham

CHAPTER 1

Possibilities for Growth

ARN Today we are seeing mounting interest in church growth. How would you explain this?

McGAVRAN Partly by the fact that many individual congregations and denominations are experiencing growth. As other churches and denominations see this, they say, "This same growth could be available to us." Furthermore, a period in which the church was being ruthlessly attacked, blamed for almost everything, is ending. Men are seeing that other plans are simply inadequate. They are turning to Christ as the only Way and realizing that the church must grow. If basic human problems are to be solved and basic needs met, the church must see the possibilities, seize the opportunities, and do a tremendous job of multiplying congregations across this land.

ARN A new spirit is penetrating some areas of the church today. Do you feel we have passed the period of negative attitudes and are moving into one of positive attitudes and possibilities of growth?

McGAVRAN Yes, I think we are leaving behind the pessimistic postwar era and are coming to a happier and a more honest age. We're seeing that the church of Jesus Christ, with all its imperfections, is a most potent factor in creating good neighborhoods, good cities and a good civilization.

ARN And what are the possibilities of church growth before us?

McGAVRAN We stand on the edge of a real surge of growth. I am not speaking about an improved spiritual condition in the church—that also will take place—but an active reaching out and winning people to Jesus Christ and multiplying cells of Christians.

ARN You're saying that if in any community there is a living church, and if in that community there are also non-Christian people, there is opportunity for growth?

McGAVRAN Unquestionably! But, of course, someone will say, "Wait a minute. These people are utterly indifferent to the church." My answer to that is that the indifference may be in *us* rather than in *them*. If we believe that these people are not going to be interested, then perhaps *for us* they won't be! But they are basically receptive. Again and again, around the world, as I have studied the growth of the church, I find communities where some new

2

church, some new denomination, some new congregation, even some new person coming in, finds a responsiveness that the older group didn't find. I can only conclude that the responsiveness was there all along.

ARN   Around the world, yes, but what of the responsiveness in America?

McGAVRAN   The American scene is fundamentally responsive. You do not have here an organized, entrenched hostility to the Christian faith such as you have in Russia, Arabia and many other countries. Here, by and large, it's considered a rather good thing to be a Christian. I think we can count on continued responsiveness in America.

ARN   And responsiveness, if properly understood, can mean growth.

McGAVRAN   Responsiveness means growth, *if* it is cared for; *if* we cultivate a fertile field, *if* we sow it, weed it, and reap it, we'll have a harvest!

SEEING THE POSSIBILITIES

ARN   And these possibilities are all around us if we but look, see, and determine to do something about them?

McGAVRAN   Yes, the possibilities for growth in the average American city are fantastic. There are pockets of population which are completely untouched. There are people in desperate need of the Gospel. People who are lonely. People whose lives are being ruined because they don't know the Lord Jesus. The potential for church growth in most places is amazing.

ARN   Suppose I'm the pastor of a church which isn't

3

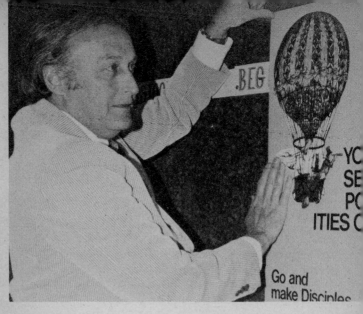

"But the first step is to see the possibilities!"

growing. Is there any hope for me? Can my church grow?

McGAVRAN The answer to that must be in the positive affirmative. Of course it can! The opportunity is there! Now there are difficulties, of course. But the opportunities for growth are very considerable.

ARN You're telling me that any church can grow if it has a will to grow and if it is preaching the gospel to needy people?

McGAVRAN If the church is preaching the good news of God's power to needy people, if it is *concerned* about church growth, if it is *thinking* about church growth, if it is *praying* about church growth, if it *enlists* people in the growth of the church, there is no reason why it shouldn't grow. You see, *God* wants His lost children *found.*

ARN But the first step is to see the possibilities.

4

McGAVRAN That's right. Possibilities! You've got to see the possibilities and believe in the possibilities. At least part of the difficulty, part of the reason for the lack of church growth, is that too many Christians have settled for *no* growth. They have concluded within themselves that growth is quite impossible, so why work for it? Once that happens, there is *no* possibility of growth.

ROADBLOCKS

ARN Now if the potential is there, why is it that so many people and so many churches have not seen the possibility and done something about it?

McGAVRAN So many Christians have become accustomed to, preoccupied with, their own congregation. They like their own congregation. That's perfectly natural. They should. But unfortunately, the outsiders remain *outsiders*. There is no way of reaching these outsiders when a church is preoccupied with its own members. So congregation after congregation is sealed off to itself, by its own language, by its own culture, by its own degree of education, or wealth, or residence. The bridges to other segments of the population, across which church growth will occur, simply are not built.

ARN Yet it is possible to build bridges; it is possible to see people open to one another and for congregations to relate to those outside in a way that leads to growth.

McGAVRAN Yes, but even before you begin to do that, other roadblocks must be cleared out of the way.

ARN Ideas such as, "But we're big enough already"; "If we grow, it is going to cost something"; "We like our church as it is"; "Why should we?"

McGAVRAN Those are common reasons for non-growth. Christians often conclude that the church exists only for their benefit. However, that is not what the Bible teaches. The church exists to glorify God. The church exists to preach the Gospel of Christ. The church exists to win the lost to salvation. As one gets back to a biblical base, and sees these things the way God sees them, he builds a theological foundation on which church growth can take place.

ARN The theological foundation causes many Americans to say, "Well, that's fine, talking about church growth, but the fact of the matter is, it is really up to God. We have little or nothing to do with it."

McGAVRAN The Lord Jesus left everything in the hands of His twelve apostles, and if they had done nothing, Pentecost would never have happened, Paul would never have made his journeys and the church would never have grown. The early Christians were very actively involved in the work of Christ and His church; they were willing to sacrifice and pay the price.

ARN You are certain there is no theological basis on which to build such non-growth excuses?

McGAVRAN There *are* no theological reasons, but plenty of theological reasons are *alleged*. These are mostly defensive thinking and rationalizations of defeat. It is necessary for deacons, elders, and preachers to recognize that defeat can be rationalized, often, in theological terms.

ARN One of the first things we must do as we're thinking about church growth, then, is to recognize that most reasons for not growing are rationalizations, or in plain English, excuses?

6

McGAVRAN Yes, if any group of men and women would sit down and check over the rationalizations that they have been accustomed to making, and that they have heard other people making, they'd do themselves a great service. Basically, churches are full of good Christians, and once they see their rationalizations, they will renounce them. It has been my experience that when you point out an excuse for non-growth, people rather ruefully laugh at themselves and clear that particular obstacle out of the way. Then they are free to see the real possibilities.

ARN What other reasons are there why churches don't grow?

McGAVRAN Sometimes indifference and sin stain a congregation. Until these are cleared out of the way, confessed and purged, nothing much is going to happen in the way of growth. Sometimes lack of growth is due to the wrong location of a church. Quite often it is due to wrong methods. But each one of these and other obstacles to the growth of a church can be recognized and cured.

ARN Not so fast! Sin and worldliness in the congregation?

McGAVRAN Yes, growth will not take place unless God's work is carried on in God's way.

ARN Wrong location?

McGAVRAN A church will grow faster if it's in a prominent location; however, don't let that be an excuse, for even a church in a poor place can experience *some* growth.

ARN Wrong method?

8

McGAVRAN Of course, thousands of churches are working hard in wrong ways and so are not experiencing growth.

ARN It's not how often you swing the ax, it's how high the woodpile grows.

GROWTH THINKING

McGAVRAN All through this book we shall be dealing with factors in the growth of the church, which, if they are neglected, will damage, arrest, or prevent church growth. Frequently growth has simply not entered into our thinking. We don't know the size of our church. We don't know how much it has grown each year for the past twenty years. We don't see the possibilities. We're operating in a fog, and this must be dissipated.

ARN Much of this fog is related to our attitudes. Attitudes, I've found, are an important ingredient of church growth. A computer analysis of fifty churches found a distinct relationship between church growth and the attitudes of the members. The members of growing churches had far more positive attitudes about their churches, program, outreach and ministry, than the average church of the survey. The declining churches had members whose attitudes were significantly below the norm. As the reader can observe from the following excerpt from the computer analysis, attitudes toward the church and its programs seem to be directly related to growth. That's why it is so important to see the possibilities, to make growth a part of your attitudes and life-style as a Christian.

McGAVRAN Churches which are not growing—and they are legion—need to wake up to the possibilities, and get a sound biblical conscience on finding the lost. Biblical

9

Excerpts from computer analysis of attitudes related to church growth among 50 churches

Attitudes Toward Church Program	Average of 50 Churches	Church A	Church B	Church C
1. Honestly now, church activities are for me . . .	%	%	%	%
(a) Burdensome	2	3	3	—
(b) Necessary duty	6	8	3	1
(c) Limited satisfaction	31	26	20	18
(d) Major source of satisfaction	61	55	65	74
2. How do you feel about the Christian Education program of your church?				
(a) Not meeting needs—ineffective	5	3	3	—
(b) Barely passing	10	12	11	—
(c) About average	48	52	49	44
(d) Meeting needs—effective	37	23	28	44
3. I find the worship services at my church . . .				
(a) Dull and uninteresting	4	7	—	—
(b) Routine	15	21	12	—
(c) Like most churches	17	12	32	7
(d) Inspiring and helpful	64	48	48	88
4. What potential do you feel your church has?				
(a) Poor	3	3	1	—
(b) Limited	10	15	10	5
(c) Average	29	47	53	—
(d) Excellent	58	30	32	91
5. Do you feel the programs being carried on by your church are . . .				
(a) Ineffective	3	3	—	—
(b) Partially effective	19	38	19	5
(c) Moderately effective	49	47	65	44
(d) Very effective	29	7	14	41
6. Which one major emphasis do you feel should receive more emphasis in your church?				
(a) Bible study—Christian Education	45	40	48	28
(b) Evangelism	27	24	17	26
(c) Missions—home and foreign	8	2	10	7
(d) Social involvement and concern	20	8	15	15

*Percentage totals in churches A, B and C do not add to 100% because all answers were not completed by all the individuals involved.

Church Membership

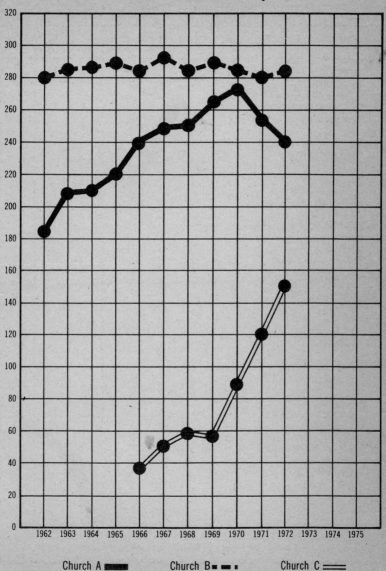

Church A ▰▰▰▰ Church B ▰ ▰ ▪ Church C ═══

convictions direct believers to work for the growth of the church. Mostly, I think churches need to realize that the growth they have been wanting, hoping for and even praying for in a vague way, is theirs if they will only do the right things. The church, as it exists in community after community, is sitting on the edge of great growth, provided it will do the right things.

ARN What do you mean by right things?

McGAVRAN It's partly method. It's partly attitude. It's partly theological positions. It's partly prayer. But most of all, it is recognizing that God wants the church to grow; that the church was made for growth; that it's normal for the church to grow and increase, and to bring people to a knowledge of salvation.

ARN And a church that is not growing would not be effectively carrying out Christ's commands.

McGAVRAN Yes. A Lutheran friend of mine says lack of growth is a disease. Fortunately, it is one that can be cured. Lack of growth must be recognized as a disease and treated. We must not believe, if our church is not growing, that this is normal and God is pleased with us. This is not true!

RESPONSIBILITY? EVERYBODY'S!

ARN In a church, growth is whose concern?

McGAVRAN *Everybody's!* Churches which are not growing are usually churches in which the responsibility for growth is all loaded onto one person, usually the minister. On the other hand, a church where everybody is working for growth, where everybody is concerned that the Gospel be known, that is a church which grows. Where everybody works at getting obstacles out of the way, where everybody learns as much as possible about the growth of the church, where the church board or session spends half its time planning for church growth, there church growth occurs.

ARN I recall very few board meetings where the subject of church growth was discussed. Is my experience common?

McGAVRAN Quite common, but it should not be. Every church board should spend hours every year, maybe hours every month, considering the growth of the church. *Planning* for it, *praying* for it, *measuring* it, and laboring in places where growth can be had is perhaps the main business of the church board.

ARN I wonder how many boards recognize growth as church business?

McGAVRAN I am afraid not too many. As a missionary, I one time fell to thinking about the number of hours our mission executive committee had spent talking about the growth of the church in India, for which the mission had been placed there. As I looked back over twenty-five years, I had to admit with considerable chagrin that we had not spent much time on church growth.

ARN That parallels my experience, not on the mission field, but in churches here in America. A church board will discuss many aspects of the ministry but seldom, if ever, discuss growth, and this is the very heart of what God would have us do. As a board member, I can see how I have failed by not keeping growth before my co-workers.

13

McGAVRAN Some of the many aspects of growth should be on the agenda of every meeting of the church board, because as long as multitudes are living and dying without the Saviour, growth is what the church exists for. The church betrays those in need if she does not bring them to the Saviour, and there are so many who, without Jesus, are ruining their lives. So many!! So many!!

OPPORTUNITIES

ARN All these unchurched, lost people mean growth possibilities, don't they? How would you illustrate this?

McGAVRAN There is a wonderful illustration in Southern California. Until 1937 California was regarded as the province of the Northern Baptists, who now call themselves the American Baptists. The Southern Baptists consequently were not actively planting churches there. In 1937, however, seeing the multitudes of unchurched, seeing that the Northern Baptists were not meeting the need, the Southern Baptists aggressively entered the state. At that time they had twelve Southern Baptist churches in California. How many do you suppose they have today?

ARN Seeing the possibilities and acting will bring results. How many churches today?

McGAVRAN Nine hundred ninety-two! In the course of thirty-five years they have grown from twelve to nearly a thousand, perhaps over a thousand by this time. To be sure, they had to cultivate the field. They had to pray and work, spend money, appoint evangelists, stimulate laymen to work and do all sorts of things. But the *opportunity* was there! This is what I want to stress more than anything else. We live in the midst of a very fertile land, but even a fertile land has to be plowed, sowed and cared for before

14

it will produce a crop. America is a wonderfully responsive place. Its basic receptivity is tremendous. It is full of opportunity for the planting of churches. This fact should be very widely recognized.

ARN Are the opportunities for growth greater today than they were some years ago?

McGAVRAN Far greater! America is much more winnable now than it was in the days of George Washington. There are more winnable people today, for example, than in the days of the gold rush, and not just because there are more people. There are more people, of course, but the church is so much stronger. There are so many more devoted women, so many more wonderful Christian men, and so many modern translations that make the Bible come alive. People themselves are more ready to become Christians now than they were.

ARN So, when we put it all together, we're saying that today is indeed an unparalleled day of opportunity. If we of the church but see opportunity, the future is bright.

McGAVRAN Yes, but just a word of caution! Church growth is a complex thing; it is not simple. There are principles for intelligent action. In coming discussions we shall be taking up the subject and turning it over and over, looking at it from many different angles. We shall consider different modes of church growth, different strategies, different methods. We shall consider the biblical convictions involved in church growth. As we do this, I hope the possibilities of church growth will open before us. For, complex as church growth is, if any church will study church growth, read about it, talk about it, and pray about it, that church will grow.

15

CHAPTER 2

Growing Churches of the New Testament

ARN In our consideration of church growth, what better place to begin than with the early church? Does the New Testament help us understand the how and why of this growth?

McGAVRAN Oh, yes, indeed. The New Testament speaks of, and demonstrates, tremendous church growth. In fact, the church was born in an explosive series of conversions. Before the Day of Pentecost, only 120 were meeting in an upper room; then on the Day of Pentecost, 3000 people turned to the Lord. I marvel when I think of the courage of that little band of inexperienced apostles in baptizing 3000 people in one day.

Those first ten wonderful chapters in the book of Acts tell of notable church growth, for example, in Acts 2:41, "And the same day there were added to them about three thousand souls." In 2:47 we read, "And the Lord added

17

to the church daily such as were being saved." In 4:4 we read, "and the number of them which believed was about five thousand men." If you add 5000 women and 5000 children, there were 15,000 believers in Jerusalem in a relatively short period of time.

Later in that fourth chapter we read, "The multitude of them that believed were of one heart and one soul." They counted them not by congregations, but by *multitudes*! I don't know how many a multitude is, but it must be a considerable number of people.

ARN   There certainly *was* growth taking place.

McGAVRAN   Much growth! In Acts 5:14 we read, "And believers were the more added to the Lord, multitudes of both men and women." Talk about women's liberation; they paid attention to it way back there—multitudes of men *and* women. We've been talking about *"added* to the Lord," but listen to this. Chapter 6 records, "And the Word of God increased; and the number of disciples *multiplied* in Jerusalem greatly" (v. 7). From *addition* to *multiplication!* Another important event was that "a great company of the priests were obedient to the faith." Up to that time the Christians had been the common people, the rank and file, the poorer element. Then, after a period of time—we don't know exactly how long—a multitude *of the priests* became obedient to the faith. That was a great day!

In chapter after chapter, we read of growth taking place. I won't refer to all the examples, but let me call your attention to Acts 9:35, where we read about two whole villages, Lydda and Sharon. The Word says that "all they that dwell at Lydda and Sharon saw him and turned to the Lord." There was not a man, not a woman, not a child, who didn't turn to the Lord in those two towns. Well, that's the kind of growth that was going on in

18

the New Testament. You will remember that when Samaria became Christian, the word that got back to the apostles was, "All Samaria has turned to the Lord." Yes, church growth occurred in a very big way in the New Testament.

REASONS FOR GROWTH

ARN We've established church growth in the New Testament, but what were the reasons which brought about such growth?

McGAVRAN There were many reasons. A principal one was God's purpose—His ongoing, unshakable, unchanging purpose—for the salvation of men. The growth and expansion of the church throughout the world does not take place in and of itself. It is God's will that this should happen. Indeed, the entire Bible from beginning to end bears testimony to God's purpose to save men. *That* underlies the church expansion recorded in the New Testament.

ARN So it was a unity of purpose to which the early church was totally committed, God's purpose of bringing men to Himself.

McGAVRAN Yes, this one unifying purpose motivated the apostles and the new Christians. It was shared by everyone who was baptized in the name of Jesus. We may say that the growth of the church was dependent upon men coming to feel about salvation the way God feels about it, and yielding themselves to God as ready instruments for His will.

ARN That is still the heart of church growth today. This is where the battle is won or lost.

McGAVRAN Another important reason for the New Testament church growth was the expectation of the Jews. They were looking for the Messiah, the Saviour of Israel. Peter and the other apostles proclaimed that He whom you have been expecting has, in fact, come.

Then, there was the Resurrection. Think what an impact the Resurrection made in Jerusalem! The man whom everybody knew had been crucified was alive and was seen by the apostles and others. The Resurrection excited enormous interest. Combine this with the expectation of the imminent return of Christ, and you have an intense fever of excitement there in Jerusalem.

ARN It's been my observation that today a church which evidences concern for men and is excited about its mission is a church that has a foundation for growth.

McGAVRAN Yes, and I'd like to add another reason, that the message was proclaimed by common people. The Pharisees, you know, said of Peter and John and the other apostles that they were ignorant and unlearned men, just ordinary people—laymen. They didn't have theological degrees. This factor, no doubt, gave their message added power. Remember, after the Day of Pentecost occurred and 3000 people were baptized and received the Holy Spirit, there were not just 12 apostles preaching, but *3000 Christians* preaching.

ARN How marvelous! God using ordinary people in an extraordinary way. He empowered these Christians to go forth.

McGAVRAN Empowered Christians who were in living contact with other people. Just think how many Jews were relatives of these new Christians. Of the 3000 who were baptized, each person must have had 50 or more relatives.

20

Soon thousands and thousands of people said, "My cousin, my uncle, my aunt, my grandfather, my grandson has now become a Christian." That was the word that filtered out. With one leap Christianity had become a real option. Following Christ had been opened to a very large number of Jews. The importance of the new convert in propagating the faith simply cannot be overestimated.

ARN Let's look at this matter from a different perspective: How do you see the role of the church in God's plan of redemption?

McGAVRAN Oh, the church is absolutely central to God's plan of redemption. Christ Himself, you know, gave the church a key role. He said, "I will build my church, and the gates of hell shall not prevail against it." The church is Christ's Body, and it must be given a very important role in the Christianization of the world.

ARN How, then, do you see the interrelationship of individual believers and the church?

McGAVRAN Well, the individual believer is a saved person. He knows Christ. He can pass on his faith. But unless the individual believer forms part of the church, he soon tends to lose his effectiveness. He grows cold and like a coal separated from the fire, soon turns black. The individual Christian separated from the church soon ceases to be an effective Christian. So the church, it seems to me, is an essential part of God's plan of salvation for the world.

ARN But in God's plan of redemption, is the emphasis on the individual or on the church?

McGAVRAN Both! God unquestionably calls individuals to believe on Him and be saved, but as soon as they do

21

Artist's conception of a New Testament house church.

believe, it is His evident purpose that they be organized into churches and function as churches. It is only in churches that we see the Word of God growing and multiplying. And wherever in the New Testament, people are converted, you see churches being instituted.

PROBLEMS OF GROWTH

ARN Meanwhile, the early church with its great growth had some problems.

McGAVRAN After Pentecost, consider just one problem. Where would the church meet? Three thousand had been baptized, and Scripture records that they continued in the fellowship, the teaching of the apostles, the breaking of the bread and prayer. Well, where did they meet? My assumption is that they didn't meet in one place. These 3000 divided up into maybe scores of meetings, at each of which Christians were instructed, partook of the Lord's

Supper, worshiped, praised God, prayed and had fellowship one with another. After Pentecost, house churches, some large, some small, broke out all across Jerusalem. That seems reasonable to me. In fact, it is the only structure which could have enabled the church to meet regularly in the weeks and months following Pentecost as Christians multiplied.

FOUNDATIONS FOR GROWTH

ARN   In these house churches, no doubt, instruction in the faith was given. I wonder what biblical foundations encouraged growth in these New Testament churches?

McGAVRAN   First, we must realize that the growth of the church took place in the midst of the Jewish people. They knew that they were the people of God. Because they were the people of God, they responded to the message. The message could have been preached to the Hindus, to the Latins, to the Anglo-Saxons, or to others who were not so prepared, but they would have rejected it. When the message of God's love was preached to the Jews, there had been prior preparation.

ARN   You mean the Jews displayed a readiness to hear the Gospel?

McGAVRAN   Yes! They were looking for the Messiah. They were accustomed to a God who speaks and acts righteously. The Jews were intended by God to be the seedbed of the church. The Holy Spirit encouraged the church to grow strong among the Jews so that it could break out to other people.

ARN   Certainly the words and demonstrations of Jesus were most significant.

23

McGAVRAN These, no doubt, had great influence. For example, many who became Christians on the Day of Pentecost must in the preceding years have seen some of the miracles recorded in the Gospels. In fact, some of them must have been directly involved. I wonder if Lazarus wasn't there on the Day of Pentecost. The apostles must have remembered the miraculous draught of fishes when they weren't expecting any fish, and the Lord said, "Throw in your nets." Man! They pulled out fish till the nets broke! On the Day of Pentecost that miracle of the nets and fishes must have come flooding back into the minds of those apostles.

ARN What a dramatic visual demonstration and fulfillment of Christ's words, "Follow me, and I will make you fishers of men."

McGAVRAN Yes, and have you ever thought that when He said these words, He wasn't talking to men who had just pulled out one lone trout which had snapped at a fly, but to men who had hauled out a net full of squirming, wriggling fish? That is when He said, "I will make you fishers of men"—not fly fishers, but net fishers.

As the disciples recalled the parables of the lost sheep, the lost coin, and the lost son, they must have thought of many lost members of their own families, and many lost neighbors. As the shepherd searched for the sheep, and as the woman searched for the lost coin, so they were going to search for these dear lost ones of their own circle. Here, and in other illustrations, as the church multiplies, we see, reflected, the words of the Lord Jesus.

BLOSSOMING CHURCHES

ARN Let's turn to some of the New Testament churches which bloomed where they were planted.

24

McGAVRAN One of the churches which grew significantly and played a very important part in the expansion of Christianity was the church at Antioch. Antioch was where the New Testament church first jumped the culture barrier. Up to that time, only Jews had become Christians, but at Antioch some laymen, not knowing any better, I suppose, started to talk "to the Greeks also" about the Lord Jesus. Now, the Greeks were uncircumcised; they ate pigs, and they had statues of naked women in their gardens. Nevertheless, laymen talked to them about Jesus Christ. The preachers would have known better; those laymen didn't. Yet when the laymen presented Christ, the Greeks believed, the Holy Spirit fell on them, and they became good Christians despite the fact that they still ate bacon for breakfast.

The Church at Antioch began to grow among both the Jews and the Gentiles. It grew so much that when the apostles heard about it, they sent Barnabas to check on the queer business. Barnabas found that the church *was* growing among the Gentiles as well as the Jews. The ministry was larger than Barnabas could handle, so he went to Tarsus and brought Saul back with him. For a year they had a wonderful experience. The record says that these churches grew very greatly. Many little congregations sprang up throughout the great city of Antioch.

ARN Well, that's a blossoming church!

McGAVRAN That blossoming church didn't confine itself to Antioch. It started sending out missionaries, another reason why it was so notable.

ARN That's a good illustration of a church which grew both by adding converts and by planting other churches.

McGAVRAN Then there was that little church at

Berea. When the apostles were forced to leave Thessalonica, they came to Berea. There the apostles gave the message, and the whole synagogue believed. It is always desirable for a community to come to the Lord as a community. The synagogue community turned en masse to the Christian faith and became a strong church.

ARN Let's explore that thought. Is it always desirable for a community to make this type of commitment?

McGAVRAN Yes, because the community comes in with little social dislocation. Everybody benefits. You don't have Christians against non-Christians. *All* have become followers of the Way. It makes for a better community. It's a good thing to have happen, and a good thing to strive toward.

ARN I find this very interesting and relevant for today, but let's consider other growing churches in the New Testament.

McGAVRAN Well, take Philadelphia mentioned in the early chapters of The Revelation. Philadelphia was marked by obedience and service and an open door. That church must have been a lovely fellowship. Then, I must mention churches at Ephesus and Corinth, Alexandria and Rome. Think of the church at Rome! What a wonderful growth that had!

We must recognize that the church grew in urban centers. The church grew strong in the great cities of the ancient world and must grow strong in the cities of North America. The New Testament tells, for the most part, about city churches. The church grew under city conditions. We can take courage from the fact that the church grew strong in the cities when it wasn't wealthy, and there were no church buildings. Christians met in homes. There was no printed New Testament. Followers of Christ were persecuted from time to time. Nevertheless, the living Lord led these early urban believers, and their churches multiplied.

ARN If there has been a contemporary trend, it's been to move churches from the city to the suburbs. Are you hinting that cities today offer opportunities for the message of Christ, opportunities not yet realized?

McGAVRAN There is no question about it. The great cities of North America have been, and are going to remain, great citadels of the church. City people need Christ just as much as anybody else. The fact that cities have power and are centers of learning, commerce and manufacturing, means that the church should concentrate upon urban church growth.

"WILTED" CHURCHES

ARN Not all of the churches in the New Testament developed their full potential. To get an accurate picture, we should discuss some of these.

McGAVRAN I suppose you are thinking of churches like Laodicea, Ephesus and Thyatira.

ARN Yes, I walked through the ancient ruins of Laodicea and saw the old pipes where the water ran from Hierapolis some six miles away to Laodicea. John wrote to the Laodicean Christians, "You are neither hot nor cold, but only lukewarm to be spewed out of the mouth." I wondered about that church and what had really happened there. Then I found a clue. It is in the letter Paul wrote to the Colossians. At the conclusion of the letter, Paul asks that his words be read to those at Laodicea. He urges Ar-

27

chippus to be diligent in the Lord's business. Perhaps even when Paul wrote, decay was beginning and years later, when John wrote, had resulted in lukewarmness.

McGAVRAN You may be very right. Whenever Christians fail to be about God's business and fail to do the things that are so clearly taught in God's word, then their churches begin to decay and fall away from God. They, also, become neither hot nor cold—like the church at Laodicea. Then there was Ephesus.

ARN At one time very strong.

McGAVRAN Very strong, but the apostle John said, "You have left your first love, and think from what a height you have fallen." This also is a sobering message to congregations today.

ARN Hmm! Ephesus was orthodox, hard-working, but left its first love. Surely the churches of the New Testament that didn't reach their potential should raise sobering thoughts in us.

McGAVRAN Thyatira fell into sin. A church cannot grow on that kind of a foundation. The church must be a pure church.

ARN But even in growing churches there were problems with individuals. Apparently Paul felt that these individuals tended to inhibit the church's potential.

McGAVRAN Ananias and Sapphira must have given the Jerusalem church quite a jolt. The sin in Corinth—the jealousy, strife and sexual immorality Paul saw there—no doubt damaged the church.

28

ARN Should we wait until a church is free from sin before we think about growing?

McGAVRAN No, I don't think we can. That's not the New Testament model, either. The New Testament church rebuked sin—in some cases excommunicated those who had sinned and refused to repent. In other cases it led sinners to repentance and brought them back into the right way, but throughout it all, the church simply went on preaching Christ. As Paul says so effectively, "We preach not ourselves and our failures. We preach Christ who, despite a degree of imperfection in our achievements, does bring men and women to new life in Him." (See 2 Cor. 4:5.) That's what the Gospel is all about.

ARN In the early church, persecution was common. Do you believe that the blood of the martyrs is the seed of the church? In other words, does persecution help or hinder church growth?

McGAVRAN Persecution has often helped church growth, and sometimes hindered church growth. It depends a great deal upon how serious and severe it is, and upon the degree of faith and courage of the Christians. There are occasions in which persecution has dampened the church and a few cases in which persecution has wiped the church out completely. But on the whole, churches are tough; they thrive on persecution. As I view the North American scene, I sometimes wonder if a little persecution here wouldn't do us good. We have it so easy, that we are not keyed up to do our best.

THE APOSTLE PAUL— CHURCH MULTIPLIER

ARN When I think about the New Testament and the

The apostle Paul teaching in the synagogue.

growth of churches, my mind focuses on that great multiplier of churches, the apostle Paul. What characteristics do you see that made him so effective in this field?

McGAVRAN Paul was a great churchman, a great multiplier of churches, a great evangelist, a great Christian. Underneath it all, he had a tremendous passion for the salvation of men. His life had been so transformed by his knowledge of Christ that he wanted everybody to share in this treasure. He counted everything else as useless, as trash, compared with the excellency of knowing Jesus Christ.

ARN He was a man of one purpose—"This one thing I do."

McGAVRAN He had unwavering purpose! He had God's message for men, and intended to deliver it. Paul was a terrifically hard worker. He couldn't be stopped. Think of the obstacles—beatings, starvation, imprisonment! Through them all, he lived courageously and victoriously. His life rebukes those of us who allow small obstacles to turn us from our course.

ARN A rebuke, yes, but also an encouragement and a model that we can follow.

McGAVRAN Yes! In his personal experience, he demonstrates how available divine power is through a constant contact with the Lord. Paul was a glorious man!

ARN Do you feel that Paul, as a multiplier of churches, had a deliberate plan?

McGAVRAN Yes, Paul had a deliberate plan, and I think I know where he got it. Up in Tarsus, he may not have been successful in planting churches. At least, in the New Testament we don't hear a word about them. However, when he came to Antioch, Paul saw the churches there growing according to the Antioch plan; that is, they grew around the synagogue communities. The Jews in the synagogue believed; then the proselytes in the synagogue believed. The proselytes were Gentiles who had become Jews. In every synagogue there were devout persons who hadn't become Jews, but, who, nevertheless, liked Jewish worship. These people could not bring themselves to follow some of the Jewish laws, but they appreciated Jewish monotheism and high ethical standards. When Paul preached Christ many "devout gentiles" believed and were baptized. That was the Antioch pattern.

After Antioch these were the communities that Paul always sought out. He always went to the synagogue. It was a remarkable thing that, although he was the Apostle to the Gentiles, he went to the synagogues first. In the synagogue he found those Gentiles who were already inclined to the Gospel.

ARN Now *that's* the principle! Look for people already inclined!

McGAVRAN If we Christians look for those whom God has prepared, we will find the most responsive and winnable people. At any rate, that is what Paul did. He went to cities, not because they were cities, I think, but because there were synagogues there.

Another thing Paul did, although the New Testment only hints at it, was to contact relatives of Christians. Paul would baptize maybe half, maybe nine-tenths of the members of the synagogue. These converts, in turn, would say to him as he prepared to leave, "Down the road you'll come to another synagogue where my sister or my mother is," or, "I have a cousin who sells rugs there, or makes tents there." Even before Paul arrived in a community, he had advance word of many approachable people; for example, in the sixteenth chapter of Romans, many verses describe men and women he knew before reaching Rome.

Where did he get this information? He got it from people who were already Christians. He was constantly reaching, not into communities where he knew no one, but into those where he already had contacts. That, by the way, is a very good principle for evangelism today. Reach your *contacts*.

FAMILY UNITS

ARN Now, you were saying something else I think we should underscore—family units. Do you see in the New Testament a pattern for winning families?

McGAVRAN It's an extraordinary thing that, as you read the Book of Acts and the Epistles, again and again you find whole families accepting Christ. You read, "He and his household believed," or, "He and his household were baptized." As the church grew, it grew by accession of families—sometimes several families acting together, sometimes one family acting alone. Think about the family of the jailer at Philippi. On the other hand, think of the gathering at the house of Cornelius, where maybe 10, 15, 20, or 30 families believed—all acting together. The Holy Spirit fell on all of them, and they all became Christians. So, the pattern in the New Testament is not that of individuals one by one accepting the Lord; it is rather that of family by family. We should appropriate this important point from the New Testament.

ARN I'm inclined to think that our Protestant heritage has been more concerned with individuals than with families! This emphasis remains today.

McGAVRAN We're living in a terribly individualistic age, when family bonds here in America are very weak. The industrial revolution of the last century, the mobility of the American family, the American business world, and our own political philosophy—all of these have contributed to individualism, rank individualism, harmful individualism. But I don't like to contrast the individual and the family as if they were irreconcilables. On occasion, individuals come to Christ. On occasion, families come to Christ. What I am saying is simply that if you can win a whole family, it is better than if you pull someone out of the family. Occasionally, however, you have to take one lone person. The rest of the family doesn't believe, and it is better to win one person than not to win any. But it is a wonderful thing when a whole family believes on the Lord Jesus.

ARN Your point is well taken, and I can illustrate it in the Sunday School movement in America. If a church brings in only children, many of them are going to fall

33

away. But if the entire family can be reached as a unit, the stability of the converts will be much greater. Innumerable bits of evidence prove that truth.

McGAVRAN Yes, I am quite sure that every effort we make to win whole families is effort in the right direction. When we concentrate on individuals, we are adopting the second best procedure.

PRINCIPLES OF GROWTH

ARN That's a good New Testament principle. Let's discuss other principles for use in establishing new churches.

McGAVRAN Undergirding all the growth of New Testament churches was a fervent faith in Jesus Christ. The church believed He had come, lived a victorious life, died on the cross for people's sins, risen again, and would return soon. There was a fervent belief in Jesus Christ.

Another principle concerned lay leadership. The church grew because laymen told others about the good news. (Remember, the church entered Antioch on the feet of laymen.) Men of Cyprus and Cyrene—we don't even know their names—got to Antioch and started the church there. The church of Rome was started by laymen. When Paul got there, he found four functioning congregations started by laymen. Laymen would preach the Gospel. Laymen would baptize new believers. Laymen would instruct new believers. That's the second principle: much lay leadership.

There was also great sensitivity to the Holy Spirit. Again and again, throughout the New Testament, the part played by the Holy Spirit is heavily emphasized.

We must see the New Testament church as an assemblage of house churches. This didn't mean that if there were 20 or 30 house churches in Corinth, the church was fractured. Paul always speaks about it as one church, the church in Corinth. It was one church even though it met in many different places. As archaeologists dig back into those early cities, they find no church foundations before A.D. 160. That means for the first 120 years, Christians met exclusively in houses, and this was a great advantage to the church. It met in many different circumstances. It wasn't burdened with the need to build churches. It gave a large number of people the opportunity to lead. "A church" was not a congregation of 5000, 2000, or even 200. A church was an assemblage of 15 or 20 people or, at the most, 30 people. Everybody knew everybody else; they cared for everybody else. It was a household of God.

There are many other principles, but I would like to stress these as we look back to New Testament days.

GIFTS FOR GROWTH

ARN The apostle Paul speaks of individual gifts in the Body of Christ. How did you see these gifts related to church growth?

McGAVRAN They are essential for church growth. The New Testament emphasizes that God gives gifts to men. Twenty-four separate gifts, all given by the Holy Spirit, are mentioned in the New Testament.

ARN Do you think gifts not mentioned in the New Testament are available in the church today?

McGAVRAN I am sure this is the case. God is not limited to twenty-four. He has infinite power and gives abilities as the need arises. Christians work not in their own strength but in the strength God provides. One of the things we have to do today is to recover our faith in God's purpose for our lives, and surrender to that. We must cheerfully accept the gifts that He gives us. Different people are given different gifts, but they are *God's* gifts. That is the important thing.

ARN   Is there a gift, do you feel, for planting churches?

McGAVRAN   Yes, and it is much more common than we think. Many people have a gift, or a combination of gifts, which enables them to communicate the gospel, and bring into existence a Christian cell that wasn't there before. God gives gifts necessary to reproduce churches and to multiply churches whenever Christians are ready to receive them.

ARN   Does that mean that the work of church building then depends only on gifted people?

McGAVRAN   I'd put it a little differently. I'd say that the work of planting churches is so important that God gives gifts along these lines to a multitude of people, to whoever is ready to receive these gifts.

ARN   So, you are saying that each individual in the church has a gift or gifts, and he or she should expect many of these gifts to be related to the ongoing work of Christ in building His church?

McGAVRAN   Exactly! Because you would misuse Christ's gifts if you used them solely for the service of existing Christians. That is not why these gifts are given. As we see God's overwhelming concern for the salvation of men, we must assume that His gifts are given to men, at least in large part, that the lost may come to know Him, whom to know is life eternal.

36

UNITY AND DISUNITY

ARN We're speaking of growing churches in the New Testament. I believe that the New Testament churches exhibited a sense of community, of caring, oneness and love, which provided the cement to hold the growing church together. What is your feeling about this, and how do you see this affecting churches today?

McGAVRAN There is no question at all that the early church had this feeling of love and unity. Christians held all things in common. When non-Christians looked at Christians, they said, "Behold, how they love one another." Love was there all right. But we must not imagine that there was no friction. Right from the beginning plenty of friction irritated the church. Some people didn't get along with other people. Even Paul and Barnabas, and Paul and Peter, had their differences. The letters of Paul to Corinth are ample evidence of friction. Despite all this, unity, oneness, love for the brethren, flowed from Christ the great Head of the Church.

ARN Churches can grow despite friction. Right?

McGAVRAN One of the standard ways churches multiply is to divide and grow. It is remarkable the number of churches that have started in "splits." Now I don't advocate splits as a way of growing, but many churches have split, and both parts grew. Christians should strive for as much unity as possible, but realize that growth can go on despite disunity and friction. The important thing is that we see the necessity of communicating Christ.

ARN And even to foster unity in a local church, one of the most wholesome things would be to engage in goal-centered outreach and growth.

McGAVRAN I wholeheartedly agree. In fact, that would probably unite a church faster and better than any one thing. Everybody would be working toward a common goal.

INTO ALL THE WORLD

ARN The great commission commands us to go into all the world. Do you see the church as a basis for evangelism in the world?

McGAVRAN Yes, and I see practically no other basis. The church, or rather the Christians, are the very ones who are evangelizing the world. Para-church organizations—like interdenominational missionary societies—rest on the church. The churches support them. The churches pray for them. The churches generate the young people who dedicate their lives to the propagation of the gospel. Back of every successful missionary, there is usually a church in which he grew to Christian manhood or Christian womanhood. The successful missionary, as he goes abroad, begins new churches. The role of the church in the evangelization of the world is very great.

ARN When do you feel we'll have the world evangelized?

McGAVRAN Some people answer: when everybody has heard. I think that's rather superficial. I like to say it is not when everybody has heard from a foreign witness who proclaims the message in a heavily foreign accent. Rather evangelization will be complete when in every part of every country a church is established in every community. When in every community you have 15 or 20 or 200 Christians (when a proportion of the community has become Christian), then everybody can hear the gospel from his own intimates, in his own tongue, and see it demonstrated. When that happens, then everybody will have a real chance to become a Christian.

CHAPTER 3

Discovering Responsiveness

ARN Do you believe that thoughtful Christians these days are greatly concerned that their own churches grow?

McGAVRAN Yes, and what's more, few churches experience real growth without real *concern* on the part of the members. Knowledge is also required. There are many reasons for church growth, and concerned members study and talk about these reasons. Throughout this book we will discuss reasons. However, to stimulate our thinking, let me say that frequently churches grow because the Gospel is preached to a clearly receptive segment of the population where people are ready to hear it and ready to decide. When a church discovers that kind of responsiveness and preaches the Gospel, people do respond, and the church grows.

ARN In our search for responsiveness, can we assume that all around us lie *responsive areas?* And when the Gospel is presented to people in these areas, growth is likely to happen?

McGAVRAN   Yes, we all know of many examples here in the United States. Baptists, Methodists, Disciples and others have found great sections of the population which were starved for the Gospel. When the message was presented in the right way, people responded. For example, when in Minnesota and Wisconsin Swedish immigrants heard the Gospel from the Baptists, they became Swedish Baptists. The responsiveness was there, but the Gospel had to be preached in Swedish, and had to be preached by *Swedes*. Those Swedish immigrants wouldn't have affiliated with an American Baptist church. American Baptists would have found no responsiveness, but the immigrants were quite willing to become Swedish Baptists. There must be responsiveness on the part of the people and an appropriate approach on the part of the advocate.

Another reason for church growth, you'll find, is that in previously non-growing congregations, some men or women get dissatisfied with non-growth. Such people refuse to be tied to work that doesn't bring results. They intend to multiply churches. They want to bring people to Christ. They resolve that their church shall grow. Anything short of this goal is unacceptable to them. A *man* or a *woman* is often the basic reason for church growth.

HINDRANCES TO GROWTH

ARN   If there are clues to why churches grow, are there clues why churches do *not* grow?

McGAVRAN   The principal clue is that leaders become chained to non-productive work. There is always plenty of work to do in every church. Many leaders, both laymen and ministers, get tied to programs which have little to do with the propagation of the Gospel and nothing to do with finding the lost. A minister can get trapped in "splendid work whether the church grows or not."

42

ARN And laymen can be endlessly involved in "busy work," meeting after meeting, committee after committee, on and on.

McGAVRAN That's right. They can look after the church, put red carpets on the floor, pay the bills, paint the church, and attend to the various problems without concerning themselves as to whether the church is making an impact on the community or reaching the multitudes who surge around our churches and never come in.

ARN When leaders are chained to existent non-productive work, churches don't grow. Let's go on. . . .

McGAVRAN Another reason for a church not growing is that no one in the church checks what is being done against the degree of growth achieved. Nobody measures. Nobody knows for sure. The church operates in a continual fog. People are simply not conscious of growth, and, therefore, it is not measured.

Supermarkets would go bankrupt if they operated their business that way. Supermarket managers check minutely and regularly on whether the store is making a profit, and what lines of merchandise bring a return.

Churches need what I call membership accounting. Churches have financial audits, but they don't often have membership audits. That's what we need, to discover where members come from and where they go.

ARN You're saying that it's important to know a church's growth pattern and if the activities carried on are really productive.

McGAVRAN Many churches feel they are carrying on activities which may sometime or other lead to church growth. They are quite comfortable in the belief that their efforts will eventually lead to growth. Whether or not activities lead to growth right now, really doesn't matter. Once a church gets saddled with this attitude, it is almost certain not to grow. The truth is that what may lead to growth five, ten, or fifteen years from now, will very probably not lead to church growth at all. Church leaders should constantly evaluate their efforts against *results now*. We must ask, "Are we, in fact, working for results in the next six months, the next six weeks, maybe the next six days?

WITHOUT CROSSING BARRIERS

ARN   Changing focus for a moment, in your study of the world-wide growth of churches, you've stated that men like to become Christians without crossing barriers. As we seek for responsiveness, does that apply to America?

McGAVRAN   Yes, that's a general principle. It applies everywhere. I am quite sure that it applies in Los Angeles, Chicago and Miami. It applies all across the United States.

ARN   If this principle applies in America, what then are some of these barriers, and how do they affect people becoming Christians?

McGAVRAN   There are barriers of education, wealth, employment. In one part of the city live people who attend the university. In a different section are people who work in factories. There are Italian sections, Irish sections, German sections. Cities are sectioned. A church in one section need not expect people from other sections to attend.

You can't see the barriers. People will deny them. But they are there just the same. University professors will tell you that they love factory workers, and I suppose they do; but as a matter of actual fact, men who work in factories

44

don't feel comfortable when they go to a church attended largely by university professors. The sermon which gets through to university professors does not speak to men who belong to Unions. There are differences between groups of men. Barriers do exist. Men like to become Christian in their own social groupings, without crossing barriers.

ARN But haven't we been led to believe that America is a "melting pot," that we're all a big happy family, that there really are no barriers?

McGAVRAN That's a common belief, but it just isn't true. Actually many differences exist, and many people take pride in these differences. We simply have to remember that church growth must go on in the midst of them. We must come to terms with them. We must use differences for the glory of God. These barriers must not stop the propagation of the Gospel.

ARN Isn't coming to the cross itself a barrier or a "stumbling block," as the apostle Paul puts it?

McGAVRAN Oh, yes. The cross, the need to repent, to be baptized, to give up known sin—all these are biblical barriers and must remain. People must be asked to cross these barriers, and only those who do can be members of the household of God. But non-biblical barriers must not be set up. It is non-biblical barriers which we must demolish. We must make sure that we ask people to become Christians where they don't have to cross barriers of language and culture and class and wealth and style of life. Every man should be able to become a Christian with his own kind of people.

ARN It seems to me that as non-biblical, unnecessary barriers are removed, receptivity should grow.

45

McGAVRAN Yes, it should. Every church has its barriers, but many can be removed. I discussed this problem with a Methodist bishop. His churches were in industrial cities in middle America to which large numbers of poor people from Appalachia had come to work in factories. The Appalachians were not becoming members of the Methodist churches. "Why?" the bishop asked. I hazarded a guess that at least part of the reason was that Christ had so blessed the people in the Methodist churches, they'd become so decent, so law-abiding, so kindly, good and affluent, that their fellow Americans from Appalachia didn't feel comfortable in their churches. Churches needed to be established among the newcomers from Appalachia, churches in which the preachers would be Appalachians, the deacons and elders Appalachians. Everybody would then feel very comfortable with everybody else.

ARN You are suggesting that some churches will appeal to one segment of society, and other churches will appeal to other segments. Right?

McGAVRAN Yes, I think that this is true.

ARN But isn't that segregation? Churches shouldn't be this way.

McGAVRAN Pride, arrogance, exclusiveness and segregation—these truly are sins. But I am speaking about something different, about a normal, natural, innocent fact that people like to be with other people of their own kind.

ARN And they gravitate to churches of their own kind for reasons of convenience.

McGAVRAN They gravitate because it is natural and normal. Our strategy should be to have churches in every

46

segment of society; so that people of every segment, feeling quite at ease, can worship and work.

ARN Now, if I as a pastor seek to remove non-biblical barriers, does that assure greater responsiveness for my church?

McGAVRAN It helps secure it. Many other factors affect responsiveness, of course. Merely removing the barriers will not cause church growth. There must be fire . . . faith . . . prayer . . . concern. Christians must believe that men and women who do not know Jesus Christ are truly lost. But if non-biblical barriers are removed, it helps to elicit greater response. People will go where they feel at home.

A MOSAIC OF HOMOGENEOUS GROUPS

ARN Earlier in our conversation, you suggested that one of the reasons why churches grow is that the Gospel was preached to a clearly receptive part of the mosaic. Now, what you're saying is that responsiveness grows as we recognize that a community is a mosaic of many homogeneous groups.

McGAVRAN Yes. Every community has many different segments. Many different communities live within the general community.

ARN The significance of homogeneous groups must be remembered as we consider growth.

McGAVRAN Let's consider these homogeneous units. Some are ethnic. One thinks immediately of Blacks, Chicanos, Chinese and Japanese immigrants; but among Caucasians also there are many ethnic or almost ethnic

47

*"Many different communities
live within the general community."*

units. On the West coast one of the homogeneous units is made up of persons who, within the last 20 or 30 years, have emigrated from the Southern states. One can spot them immediately by their Southern accent. The existence of this enormous homogeneous unit is part of the reason for the fantastic growth of the Southern Baptist churches in California. When the Southern Baptist churches came in, these Southerners said to themselves, "Ah, here's our kind of church. The minister preaches in the right way." He may have been preaching the same doctrine as other established churches, but he was using "a good ol' Southern drawl" as he preached. It sounded good to Southerners. Southern Baptist churches multiplied.

To use another illustration, the *hippies* with their counter-culture formed a distinct homogeneous group, a unit of society most "straight" churches were utterly unable to influence. The hippies were so completely separated from normal society that they were not hearing the Gospel preached in "straight" churches all around them. Recently many churches which accept hippie culture have been started among the counter-culture people. In these, hippies feel at home. Their hair and dress style is accepted, and they feel comfortable.

ARN Where they wouldn't feel at home in a straight-line Protestant church. Could the straight-line church so adapt its services and its way of doing things that it would attract the counter-culture people? To a degree this same question arises wherever a church made up of one kind of people deliberately tries to win another kind of people. Can a church do this successfully?

McGAVRAN I think it can. Of course, the greater the gap, the more difficult it is. Many small gaps can be, and are being, successfully bridged. First, Christians must identify these gaps and determine to bridge them.

ARN Many of our denominations were founded in groups that migrated to America. The denominations became closely-knit racial and linguistic brotherhoods like the German Brethren, the Swedish Lutherans, the Old Mennonites and others. Can we expect such denominations to grow significantly?

McGAVRAN A very interesting example is the Swedish Baptist denomination. Until 1940 its members called themselves Swedish Baptists, and the members were almost exclusively of Swedish descent. Between 1920 and 1940, the church had almost ceased growing. That particular pocket of the population had been worked out. So about 1940 the Swedish Baptists turned over a new leaf. They determined to call themselve General Conference Baptists, send out large numbers of missionaries, plant churches, and proclaim the Gospel among Americans in general. They have doubled in the last thirty years, and the

49

Lord has prospered them greatly, but it took a deliberate effort on their part to do this.

A DISTINCT PERSONALITY

ARN   As I have ministered in churches, I've discovered that churches, like individuals, seem to have personalities of their own. Have you noticed this?

McGAVRAN   Oh, yes, churches have distinct personalities, both as regards denominations and within each denomination. Some churches are bright and friendly; others are not so friendly. Some are courageous; some are not so courageous. Some are sleeping, some are wide awake. Churches definitely have personalities.

ARN   It is my conviction that when a church discovers its personality; that is, its strengths and weaknesses, and builds upon its strengths, it is a stronger church. As a person is weaker when he endeavors to imitate someone else rather than be himself, so a church is weaker if it endeavors to adopt and adapt success programs of other churches —programs which are not its own. This weakness I find in many churches—not discovering and using their own God-given personalities to reach their community. Personality has something to do with growth and responsiveness.

McGAVRAN   Just as one is attracted to open, friendly, kindly persons, one is attracted to open, friendly, kindly churches. Churches perhaps more than individuals can change undesirable traits of personality. The church does not have to be introverted and cold and withdrawn. It can be open and friendly.

ARN   A congregation attracts the kind of people that it already has in it. This can seriously limit growth when there are no more of that particular kind of people in the community. When that happens, the congregation must deliberately break into other strata of society if growth is to continue. But must we limit ourselves to the responsive people like us in our own neighborhoods and cities? To do so poses a problem. If my most responsive area really is my own homogeneous grouping, how then can I effectively take the Gospel into all the world?

EVANGELISM ONE, TWO, THREE

McGAVRAN There are *three* kinds of evangelism. When one is reaching out to his own kind of people, he is carrying on "Evangelism One." He is talking to his intimates, friends, business companions, uncles and aunts, sisters and cousins; to those who belong to his club or work in his factory or office. Here unstructured spontaneous evangelism functions well.

Then in your same town there are other homogeneous units, other segments of society you seldom meet. If you invite men from one of those segments to your church, they don't come. And if they did, they would feel ill at ease because their kind of people are not there.

ARN I think we've all been in similar situations and felt rather uncomfortable.

McGAVRAN A different kind of evangelism is needed for them. Let's call that "Evangelism Two." They are still part of your town. They still speak English. They are still Americans, but they are somewhat removed.

ARN How would you suggest that a church might reach people in the community in "Evangelism Two"?

McGAVRAN To reach people living on the other side

of a culture barrier requires a conscious effort. It won't happen spontaneously. It requires deliberate evangelizing. Furthermore, when such people start to come to your church, they must be particularly welcomed, and it is most important that others of that same segment of society be won fairly rapidly. If the older members of the church go out of their way to be good to these newcomers, that helps; but it is not enough. Nobody in one segment of society can be good enough to people in other segments of society to make them feel thoroughly at home. What they need is 15, 20, 50 or 100 people of that segment of society added. Then the church becomes their church.

ARN A good way to begin "Evangelism Two" might be in home Bible studies—in smaller groupings which grow strong in that other segment of society and maintain a degree of cultural identity.

McGAVRAN Yes, precisely, because in a home Bible study or home church, the new Christians from that other segment of society could form a third, or a half of the group, and would feel less out of place. The normal processes of friendship would serve to tie this group to the church. A multitude of house churches spreading out through the community is one of the best ways of bridging that gap. And if "Evangelism Two" is really successful, it will start new churches in those other segments of society.

ARN Could you illustrate that?

McGAVRAN A recent letter from a minister friend of mine in Dallas, Texas, will illustrate the point. "My church-growth reading led me to the conclusion that the Cubans in our midst were a prime opportunity for evangelization. Our labors in their midst have proved our assumptions. We find that there is a hunger for relationships and openness to the evangelical Christian faith. My congregation has launched a five-phase plan which we hope will eventually become a self-supporting congregation. We have learned that we have a community of 1500 Cubans in the city and 2001 in the county. Surely, it is not too much to hope that we can have three or four congregations. Church Growth Eyes—the ability to think realistically about church growth—have led us to see a tremendous opportunity."

ARN What about "Evangelism Three"?

McGAVRAN "Evangelism Three" is carried on where there are differences of language and race, as well as of wealth and education. It's the kind of evangelism one does when he goes to Africa, Singapore, or Japan. For "Evangelism Three" the church must have a corps of missionaries with special training.

We evangelize our neighbors and friends in "Evangelism One"; make special efforts to reach into new communities in "Evangelism Two"; and pray that our sons and daughters will go abroad as missionaries of the gospel in "Evangelism Three." All three types are needed.

ARN Sounds like good biblical wisdom. The Word says, " . . . you shall be witnesses unto me in . . ."

McGAVRAN " . . . Jerusalem, in all Judea, in Samaria and unto the uttermost part of the earth." (See Acts 1:8.) Evangelism—one, two and three!

RESPONSE TO CHANGE

ARN Here's a question which pastors ask me. "Suppose my church were located in what was once a responsive area but over the years the community has changed? Now the community no longer seems to be responsive to the ministry which we project. Should our church stay or should we leave?"

McGAVRAN There are so many answers to that, and so many factors are concerned, that I hesitate to say anything, but let me try to give some insights. If the church no longer attracts, leaders might ask themselves if improvements in the ministry are necessary. Ministries do get into ruts. Sometimes responsiveness is there, but the methods being used don't release it. Hopefully, the church is elastic enough to change in order to fit changing circumstances. Of course, one thinks about Caucasian towns in process of becoming Chicano. In a Southern California community, older Caucasian inhabitants are selling out, and Latins are flooding in. The old Caucasian churches are dying on the vine. I've seen the same thing in Northern Michigan. The older populations there moved to the industrial cities, and the newcomers (from Southern Europe mostly) were not persuaded to become members of the existing churches. So the older churches across thirty years were wiped out.

A changing neighborhood is a difficult situation, but churches should not be wiped out. While the older churches are there, they should do their utmost, their level best, to win into themselves the new population. We'll discuss this situation later in the chapter called "Changing Church."

ARN What about the people who say, "This has been my church"? Should they give up some of the reins of power?

McGAVRAN Yes, indeed. They cannot expect other people to come into a church which they have no share in running. People not only like to become Christians without crossing barriers, but they like to belong to a church in

54

which they have a voice, in which some of them become deacons and teachers and ministers. Newcomers should be able to say with justifiable pride, "This is my church. My kind of people share in the management."

Part of the problem is this matter of giving up control. I was preaching in a little church in Northeastern Ohio, which had been there for over a hundred years. Control through the years had been vested in five or six families. Then the suburbs of a nearby industrial city came out and wrapped around this rural church. The minister tried to get people who had recently moved into the vicinity to attend, but after a few weeks, they would drop away. The trouble was, the church was controlled by half a dozen families.

When I visited there several years later, however, the church was jammed to the doors. In talking with the minister, I asked "How, did you get over the hump?"

He said, "We had a revival meeting! We took in 106 people on one Sunday, and swamped the old guard! New officers were elected, new Sunday School teachers appointed. From then on, it was the church of the newcomers." Well, that is one way of doing it.

I said, "The old guard must have been quite angry."

He said, "On the contrary, they were delighted. They were so pleased that the church had at long last really become a church of the people." Isn't that refreshing?

STRATEGY IN RESPONSIVENESS

ARN What a fine attitude! I could illustrate your point, also, as I think of the many young people in churches who are held at arm's length by the power structure. They soon drift away; but when young people are integrated into the church and assume places of leadership, it becomes their church. Let's shift the conversation to *really* non-responsive areas. How do you handle them?

55

McGAVRAN We should keep an eye on what appear to be permanently non-responsive areas. We should pray that God will turn them to Himself. Then, too, maybe they are basically responsive, and we have neglected them. The real trouble may be that we have not found the right key, or the right man to open that responsiveness! Even if they are basically non-responsive now, they may turn responsive in the future. Don't write any area off permanently. Keep praying that the Holy Spirit will transform resistant populations into receptive populations.

ARN Once we have discovered responsiveness, do you believe that good church strategy concentrates major emphases there?

McGAVRAN Yes, we should concentrate where God has ripened the field. When we find people in need, we should minister the Gospel. People do not become ripe by accident. They ripen by the purpose of God. It is true that various factors play upon them, but who produces the factors? The church is well advised to consider that responsiveness means the finger of God pointing at that population saying, "Go and bear witness there. A church is waiting to be born."

CHAPTER 4

Measuring Church Growth

ARN   A good way to begin our conversation would be to consider how churches grow.

WAYS CHURCHES GROW

McGAVRAN   Churches grow in three ways—biological growth, transfer growth and conversion growth. By biological church growth, I mean that which takes place within the family. A man and his wife who are true Christians have, let us say, three children. These grow up, confess Christ, and are added to the church. There are now five Christians. This is biological growth—good and important! The Bible commands us to rear our children in the fear and admonition of the Lord. However, biological growth will never win the world for Christ.

ARN   What growth rate in the church might be expected by biological means?

McGAVRAN This depends upon the rate of growth of the population. In some parts of the world twenty percent a decade, or two percent a year. In America, with its emphasis on family planning and limited population increase, it will be less. Growth rate also depends on the mobility of a community, but in any case, biological growth is not a large growth. A church which depended only on this growth would be committing suicide!

ARN There are too many "dead" churches now. We don't need any suicides. What about transfer growth?

McGAVRAN Transfer growth is that which takes place when people move from one area to another, from the country to the city, or vice versa. The city churches grow larger, and the rural churches grow smaller. That's transfer church growth. If I change a five-dollar bill from one pocket to another, one pocket gets fatter while the other pocket gets leaner, yet my total wealth remains the same.

ARN Transfer growth always means increase for one church and decrease for another, so there has really been no growth in the overall body of Christ.

McGAVRAN Transfer growth is good growth. We should make sure that those who leave one church are brought into the fellowship of another. However, here again, transfer growth will not win the world to Christ.

ARN Transfer growth will make a church look as if it's growing.

McGAVRAN But it's deceptive. The pastor who is simply gathering up incoming Christians and adding them to his church feels good about it, but he has not really added to the church at large.

That brings me to the third kind of church growth, which I call conversion growth, when people come to know Jesus Christ for the first time. Conversion growth is the only kind that really adds significantly to the church.

ARN   If we would grow, the focus of effort should be on winning people through conversion.

McGAVRAN   Yes, no question about it. Every church should aim for conversion growth. Even though it might have considerable increase by transfer and biological growth, a church should not be satisfied unless it is growing by conversion. Without conversions, the church in the United States will go steadily downhill.

ARN   Do you think someone might ask, "But if we go on converting people, won't we soon run out?"

McGAVRAN   A Southern Baptist friend of mine used to say expansively, when he was contemplating the spectacular growth his denomination was achieving, "Well, by 1990 there'll be more Southern Baptists in the United States than there are people!" Seriously, tremendous numbers of people are living apart from Christ. They never darken the door of a church. In some communities only ten percent of the population are practicing Christians; in others, possibly fifty percent are. That still leaves huge numbers in the United States who neither know Christ nor love Him.

ARN   Let me underscore that—if we want wholesome growth, our focus must be on people who need to know Jesus Christ.

McGAVRAN   Exactly!

ARN If there's value in knowing the ways people come into a church, there must also be value in knowing the ways people leave the church.

McGAVRAN Yes. This information is helpful because it tells where the back doors are. People leave the church through death, transfer, and falling away, and we need to know which of these is the major cause. Furthermore, we need to know what ages are losing interest and what groups are falling away. Is it the new members who join the church and within six months are gone? Or is it the youth, or the older members who no longer find the church meeting their needs? We need to know why individuals leave the church, also why groups leave. Once we have this information, we can do something about it. Until then, we have only a vague feeling that everything is not well with the church.

DIAGNOSING CHURCH HEALTH

ARN Which brings us into the important area of diagnosing church health.

McGAVRAN It's like a doctor diagnosing the sickness of a patient. Until he knows what the disease is, how can he prescribe a cure? Until the church diagnoses the difficulty, how can the problem be remedied?

Such questions as these need to be asked: In what areas is the church in poor health? What areas of the church are growing? What areas are not growing? Where is the church effective in the community? Where is it not effective? Is the church reproducing itself at various levels: the children, the youth, the young adults, the middle-aged, the business people, the single women? Information in all these areas is essential to a church. Board members and leaders in all age groups should be keenly aware of these

60

CH MEMBERSHIP

CHURCH B

65 66 67 68 69 70 71 72 73 74 75 76 77

*"Membership statistics are not
everything, of course, but they do indicate trends."*

facts. A massive amount of growth data should be available which the average member simply doesn't have.

ARN Church members cannot plan intelligent strategy without this information. They'll find themselves reacting rather than acting! In the diagnostic process, how important are membership statistics?

McGAVRAN Membership statistics are not everything, of course, but they do indicate trends. Statistics are a kind of shorthand that compress into a very small compass the information which members of the church, and leaders of the church, ought to have. This membership information is varied and useful. It is made even more useful when transferred to charts. Columns of figures are difficult to understand, but when you place those columns of figures on charts and graphs, they speak very vividly.

ARN You're suggesting, then, that a church would do

well to construct charts and graphs of the growth or decline of its membership and possibly individual departments of the church.

McGAVRAN Indeed! A few years ago I saw graphs indicating the increase of the number of planes flying between Los Angeles and San Francisco. The number of planes between these two great cities will almost double in the coming ten years. That fact means more noise, more airports, more travel and many other complications. I saw these charts for only a few minutes, but they were etched on my mind.

Why shouldn't similar figures concerning the membership be etched on the minds of all members of the church? Opinion formers, leaders, voters and people who pay the bills—all should have accurate and vivid information as to what is really happening. You see, statistics can be made into a series of vivid pictures. It is hard to understand numbers until we see them in pictorial fashion. Graphs and charts are constantly used by businessmen and by financial leaders. Similarly, Christians should make graphs of growth facts and see that they become a common experience in the life of the church.

ARN I can see where charts and graphs can be very helpful in plotting the course of a church, in seeing where a church has been and where it could possibly go; but there are some things that charts and graphs do not tell.

McGAVRAN Yes, indeed. For example, they'll tell us that a surge of growth took place in a given year, but they won't tell the reasons for this. Charts and graphs can tell us that a church has been on a plateau for a period of years, but again they won't tell the reasons. Reasons for upsurge or decline, peaks or troughs, are not given. Charts will point to the years in which something must have taken place. It is up to us to go back to other records—to histories, to what happened in those years, to changes in lay leadership or ministerial leadership, to the adoption of certain policies that worked out well or were disastrous. The charts show us where to look and are really indispensable.

ARN In looking at charts, one usually sees an unevenness of growth. What kind of growth pattern should be "normal"?

McGAVRAN Only a few churches have their denominational and local programs so well coordinated that they grow steadily year after year. The growth lines of most churches and denominations show a great deal of unevenness—up some years, down some years, with certain congregations growing, and certain congregations of the same denomination stagnating. Much of this unevenness should not be. As long as multitudes of people live in the neighborhood who are not practicing Christians, who do not have the power of Christ in their lives, the church has unlimited opportunity to grow. A church should not think that after a great surge of growth, a long plateau is a normal experience. A plateau is not a normal experience. The normal experience is for the church to grow.

ARN But unfortunately, too many churches live on plateaus and are unaware of it. Therefore, a church that uses charts will quickly know of arrested growth and apply a remedy.

McGAVRAN Gathering statistics and focusing attention on the growth of the church often induces in the whole congregation a desire to grow. It is, of course, necessary to avoid a simplistic approach. Simply to take the gross facts of growth, namely, that a congregation had 359

Church A

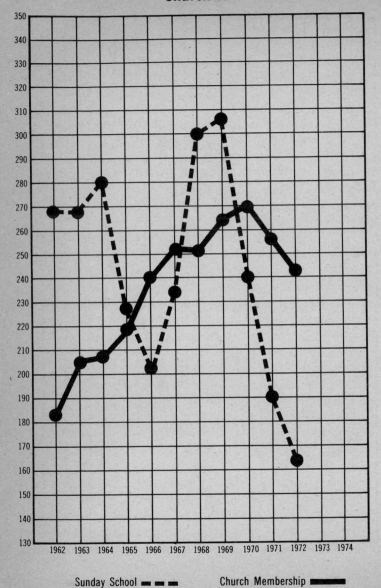

Sunday School ▬ ▬ ▬   Church Membership ▬▬▬▬

Church B

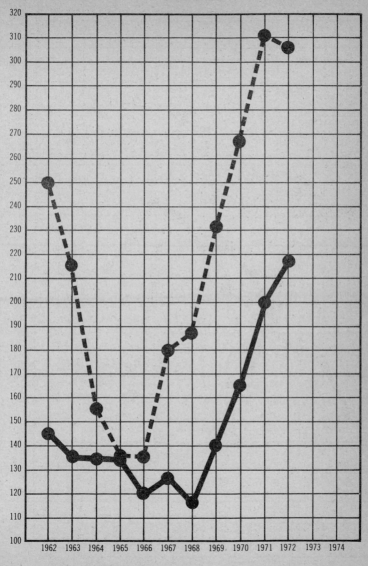

Sunday School ▪▬ ▬ ▬   Church Membership ▬▬▬▬

members and gradually came to have 421, is not sufficient. What is needed is to see the total membership broken down by age groupings, by neighborhood groupings, by family relationships, school districts, homogeneous groups, and the like. These facts must be correlated with the growth of the church if an accurate picture is to be seen.

ARN Recently I've completed an interesting study comparing Sunday School growth charts to church growth charts.

McGAVRAN What did you find?

A BAROMETER

ARN The (Sunday School) seems to be a barometer which forecasts what will happen to the growth of the church. If a Sunday School chart goes up, a church can anticipate growth. If a Sunday School chart goes down, you'll discover that for a year or two the church will hold steady; then it too will decline. This relationship is not always one to one. However, if I were a pastor and my Sunday School began to decline, I would consider it a danger signal. On the other hand, if I were interested in growth, the Sunday School might be a place to concentrate effort.

McGAVRAN I am sure that is correct. I would add this, however, that it is possible to have a Sunday School with good religious education going on, graded lessons, and well-trained teachers, which does not add significantly to the church. The crucial factor is this: if in the Sunday School classes the teachers are consciously trying to make the Sunday School an avenue into the church and are leading their pupils to become Christians and to become reliable members of the church, then the Sunday School feeds the church very well. If, on the other hand, there is not this conscious attempt, one may have a good Sunday School, but the church itself does not prosper.

ARN Our church-growth vision must include all ministries of the church: the Sunday School, women's group, men's group, youth groups. All ministries must have a consciousness that they are working together at winning people for Christ and the church. As a church identifies its goals and these are "owned" by all groups, results begin to be seen.

McGAVRAN Group effort pays dividends. A church recently came to my attention which sent out a fleet of buses and brought a large number of children to the Sunday School. The Sunday School grew very greatly, but since the parents of the children weren't reached by other groups in the church, the children seldom became permanent members. This sort of Sunday School growth proved deceptive. The trouble could have been diagnosed much earlier if the leadership of the church had asked, "Of the children who came to church last year, how many brought their parents? How many parents confessed Christ and joined the church? How many soon stopped coming?" The data brought in by these simple questions, if graphed, would have shown the facts long before the symptoms arose and an appropriate remedy could have been applied.

"HEAD COUNTING"

ARN There will be resistance to the concept of "head counting." Do you have biblical support?

McGAVRAN The Bible takes number of members very seriously indeed. Luke records numbers with great exactitude. We know, for example, that there were exactly 120 members of the church before Pentecost, and on Pentecost 3000 people accepted the Lord Jesus. The whole book of Numbers is given over to a very exact counting. This is made beautifully clear, by the way, in *The Living Bible*. The older versions of the Bible run the numbers into ordinary verses, but *The Living Bible* makes tables of them, and you have just to cast your eye over the various chapters of the book of Numbers to see how seriously the Bible takes them.

If the shepherd had not counted his sheep correctly, he wouldn't have known that there was just one that was lost. The Bible considers numbering really important. Anyone who numbers his church carefully can be sure he is doing something that is thoroughly biblical.

ARN But what of the people who say, "You can't measure God's work," or, "Leave the results to the Spirit," or "All you have to do is preach the Word"?

McGAVRAN They are partially correct. You can't measure some things, that's perfectly true. But many things can be, and indeed must be, measured. Take money, for example; what church would run without business methods, an annual audit, carefully checked bank balances and cash reserves? All of this is looked after. It must be the same with members. When God gives us saved people, when he gives sons and daughters, He expects us to look after them.

ARN You see church membership, then, as being rather significant, rather important, don't you?

McGAVRAN We must never get into the habit of playing down membership. On the contrary, we should be asking, "Is this church growing? If not, why not?" "Is our church on a plateau; is it declining?" We ask these questions, not for self-aggrandizement, but in order to do God's will better, to be more effective. In fact, as long as two men can lift more than one, church growth is important, and membership accounting is important.

MEN WHO BUILD

ARN If you were on a pulpit committee to call a new pastor, and you wanted your church to grow, what characteristics would you look for in a man?

McGAVRAN I would study the records of the men whom I considered calling. I'd look for bold men. It takes courage to launch forward in growth. I'd look for men who have a conscience on church growth. There is a great example of a Presbyterian minister. When called to a notable church in Seattle, he wrote saying, "I'll accept your call provided you understand that you and I together are going to be planting churches all over the area." When the board got that letter, they considered it carefully and came to the prayerful decision that they wanted that kind of a pastor. The net result was that this Presbyterian church fathered thirty-five other churches in the Seattle area. That's the kind of a man I'd look for if I were calling a minister.

ARN You'd look for a man who was bold, who had a record of achievement, and who would launch out on faith.

McGAVRAN Yes, one who had a conscience on the growth of the church.

ARN If you were the pastor of a church and wanted to see it grow, what kind of lay men and women would you seek for leadership?

McGAVRAN We need multitudes of laymen who have a conscience on church growth, who dig up the facts concerning the growth of the church, who draw graphs of church growth just as readily as they draw graphs of the profits and losses in their own businesses, who apply to the church the same good methods that keep their businesses operating in the black. We'll be considering qualities of good lay leadership later.

SUCCESS?

ARN In America many Christians feel that bigness is a sign of success and smallness a sign of failure. Can you apply that criterion to churches?

McGAVRAN Everything starts small. We must not say smallness is a sign of failure. I like to think of it in another light. What are we doing with the talent God has given us? To some He has given one talent, and to some He has given ten. He requires each one of us to deal responsibly with the talents He has given us to use for church growth. We must deal with our own particular opportunity. We may be located in a community where hundreds of new people come in yearly. Or we may be in a community where there are only a few new people. It would be quite unrealistic to expect the church to grow equally in both communities. It is not helpful to think of bigness as a mark of success, and smallness as a mark of failure. We must also look at the situation.

And most important, we must think of church growth in terms of obedience. The question, then, is: how obedient are we to God in the tasks that He gives us to do? How seriously do we take the lostness of men? How intent are we that our neighbors, friends, relatives and the new people who have moved in come to know Christ, His power, and His love?

70

OPTIMAL GROWTH

ARN That standard of obedience and "growing as much as you can where you're planted" seems good to me. I respond negatively to churchmen who think bigness alone is the sign of success. But that leads to another consideration. What about optimal growth and effectiveness for a church?

McGAVRAN America has a very mobile population. We won't keep all we win and consequently we must be continually winning, even to stand still. The optimal goal you mentioned, then is *steady annual increase*. Theoretically, the time might come when everyone in a community had been churched. What then? Well, every church should be a missionary church, not only evangelizing in its own neighborhood, but planting churches out beyond the neighborhoods to which people can walk or drive. Every church ought to see to it that earth's farthest bounds are irradiated with the gospel.

ARN I like what you are saying, but on a practical level, what guidelines help us know how big a church should be before it starts planting another?

McGAVRAN One finds so many different sizes of churches that no one answer will fit all circumstances. Some churches of fifty or a hundred members are glorious churches! Others of four or five hundred are also glorious! Some of six to ten thousand are wonderful churches! All that can be said, I think, is that the matter of size is one which every church should face on its own. Many of my friends are inclined to say that when a church grows to more than four or five hundred members, its members cannot know other people, and at that point it should "hive" and start other congregations.

ARN   How do you feel about that idea?

McGAVRAN   It has a great deal of truth. One of the functions of the church is to be the family of God, and you cannot love people and support them in their needs, sorrow with them in their sorrows, and rejoice with them in their joys unless you know them. Large churches must have many small compartments, churches within churches, so to speak, to be effective. Possibly with the American genius for organization, a church of thousands can be made into a federation of small intimate congregations.

ARN   Suppose it were time to "hive," how many members should there be to begin a new church?

McGAVRAN   It depends upon the kind of church you are talking about. It's quite possible to begin a house church with a dozen people who meet regularly. Such a congregation takes it from there, grows month by month, and year by year, until it builds a sanctuary. On the other hand, many churches "hive" by separating from themselves 50, 60, 100 or more members, who live in a certain area of town, and saying to them, "The time has now come for you to form yourself into a new congregation. We will aid you by buying the land, or perhaps giving you forty thousand dollars to get started. We will come over occasionally and worship with you. We'll send our choir over from time to time. We are your parents, and we are going to be praying for you and backing you up."

Both methods are effective. There is no one way of starting a church. If I were to frame a general rule, however, it would be to start a church *whenever* you can, *wherever* you can.

ARN   Whenever you can, wherever you can!! But aren't some of these newly-born churches going to fail?

McGAVRAN   Yes, some are going to fail. On the other hand, it is remarkable how tough churches are. They don't fail easily once started. Of course, one has to be practical in these matters. It would be a pity to take a good ongoing church which now assembles four or five hundred people every Sunday and break it up into a number of small, weak groups, none of which could do what the larger group accomplishes naturally. The church must grow, but it must not be fractured. Common sense is called for.

ARN   A child is born into the family, grows into childhood, through youth, then matures enough to leave home and begin a family of his own. Possibly there's a similar pattern of birth, growth, maturity and reproduction needed among churches.

McGAVRAN   Yes. And here's another thought. Many sections of a city today need a church which people can attend without driving great distances. One of the anomalies in the American scene is the large number of people who drive 5, 10, 15 miles to church. They do this for a number of reasons, but as a result, their neighborhood is left without a church. Ten families live in a row on a given street. One drives to church 7 miles in one direction, another 15 miles in another direction, a third 7 miles in still another direction. In this situation, evangelistic potency is low. It's difficult to persuade the other seven families to drive off across town to church. This weakness in the American scene needs to be eliminated in coming years.

REGULAR CHECKUPS

ARN   I assume from our conversation that you feel measuring church growth is something that should not be done once and then forgotten. Should there be periodic checkups in the body of the church?

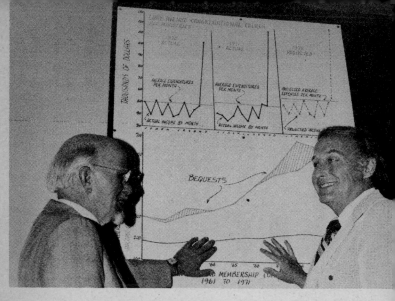

"A church concerned enough to measure where it had been, would plan where it should go, and take steps to get there."

McGAVRAN Doctors and dentists tell us of the need for regular checkups. The same is true of the church. Every church board needs to have at least an annual picture of the health and growth of the church and its various departments. In the room where the board or session meets, a large graph should cover the whole side of the room. On this would be a dozen different lines showing exact statistical pictures of a dozen significant aspects of the church, not merely how much money has been given or how large the overall membership is. Many significant aspects of the church could easily be charted month after month, quarter after quarter, and year after year. Then as the board or the session met, it could see at a glance the health and vitality of the church, and also those areas needing attention.

ARN Such a chart, or series of charts, would encourage church growth. A church concerned enough to measure where it had been, would plan where it should go, and take steps to get there.

McGAVRAN Yes, annual measurement helps promote church growth, and church growth is really just obedience to the Lord.

CHAPTER 5

Leadership for Growing Churches

NEW CONVERTS AND GROWTH

ARN "If you want your church to grow, choose many leaders from your new converts." That will be a shocking statement to many. How do you respond?

McGAVRAN New converts come from receptive segments of the population. In fact, one way to determine a receptive area is to see where converts come from. These converts are in touch with many who need the Gospel; whereas, older Christians tend to have fewer close contacts among non-Christians. New converts tend to be enthusiastic, for they don't become converts unless they have found something that really changes their lives. New converts very often witness to their friends and build up Christian groups among former non-Christian companions. Yes, new converts are the greatest source of good leaders if the church would grow. This must never be forgotten.

ARN   In the power structure of a church, do you see new converts and established members working together for growth?

McGAVRAN   Yes and No! Yes, in that it's a very natural thing to work together, for both are in the same church and have the same minister.

No, in that a new convert must not become subordinate to the older Christian. The new convert must have room to run—to grow. He must not be perpetually overshadowed by the older Christians. You see the new convert can approach his own people sometimes better alone, because he has had such close contact with them. He doesn't scare them, whereas the older Christian might. To illustrate this, think about a church with a few young people and many elderly people. Let us suppose that such a church resolved to win many youth into the fellowship. New young converts must be encouraged to enlist other young people. The task of the older adults is to help, befriend—and keep the youth group looking youthful! In that "elderly congregation" nothing would kill growth faster than to have many older people in the youth group. Do you see the point?

ARN   Yes, but carry it a step further. New converts are effective in reaching others with their enthusiasm and desire to see friends won, but do you see them being part of the boards and structure of the church?

McGAVRAN   Yes, definitely so. As they begin to play a responsible part in the church, these new members must be given an active part in the government of the church.

ARN   . . . to be part of the power structure?

McGAVRAN   Yes, it should be *their* church. They must

feel that it is their church, in which they have a voice.

RECRUITING AND TRAINING

ARN For growing churches, recruiting and training leaders is important. What plan do you propose?

McGAVRAN A good plan is one which was an essential part of the New Testament program. One secret of New Testament church growth was that leaders were trained in and by the church *in action*. It trained as it went forward. This remains a secret of church growth today. Trainees who come out of victorious churches, and have been trained by men who are themselves multipliers of churches, are generally effective. When trainees come out of cold churches that have stopped growing and are trained under academicians, their potential for church growth is limited.

ARN The most effective training, I believe, is first-hand experience. A skilled pastor or lay leader reproduces in a "Timothy" those qualities of life in Christ which are in turn reproduced in others. This training does not consist of lectures but the method of Jesus when He invited His disciples "to come and follow. . . ." The leader became the model.

McGAVRAN That sort of training of leaders marked Pastor Kennedy's work at Coral Ridge. He took people one by one and trained them to present the gospel effectively. The results in his church have been outstanding.

ARN It seems to me that both the recruiting and the training of leaders are the responsibility of the local church.

McGAVRAN Yes, certainly. The local church is obligated to train its leadership. Resources may be available through denominational or interdenominational sources, or through other churches which have worked out successful leadership training plans. But, in the final analysis, the responsibility for recruiting and training its leaders rests upon the local church. Unless it faces its responsibility, the possibilities for growth are limited.

"DISCIPLING"

ARN Do you see leadership and "discipling" as the same process?

McGAVRAN Church-growth men use the word "discipling" to mean the initial step by which people come to Christ and become baptized believers. We go on and say that the second part of church growth is "perfecting" or growing in grace. It's making sure that the baptized believers become biblical Christians, that their lives are irradiated by the knowledge of the Bible, and that they have a deep personal relationship with Jesus Christ.

In America today many Christians are interested solely in perfecting existing Christians and not in finding the lost and discipling them. This is a mistake. Mind you, I am all for Christians being better Christians. We should act more justly, and have more love for each other; nevertheless, no amount of loving each other and treating each other more justly is really going to help the church grow very much. You've got to go out where the lost sheep are. You've got to search for them in the right ravines, then get near them and persuade them to come into the fold. We need both discipling and perfecting. We need to find the lost and help them grow in grace.

ARN I've discovered that those who have found Christ

80

"To grow in Christlikeness means to share His burden for the salvation of the world."

and who actively participate in finding others are actually growing in grace. They are being perfected. They are sharing the mind of Christ more than Christians who never search for the lost. In other words, if Christians are involved in meaningful outreach, they themselves are going to grow better, faster and more effectively as Christians.

McGAVRAN I agree with you thoroughly. The thought that we can be really good Christians while not caring about the people all around about us who do not know Christ is a pernicious device of Satan.

ARN To grow in Christlikeness means to share His burden for the salvation of the world.

McGAVRAN The only way in which one can really share the mind of Christ is by getting actively involved in searching for the lost. Our Lord said on numerous occasions that He came to seek and save those who are lost. If

81

"If a church is to grow, it must equip its members for evangelism, train them to lead others to Christ."

we would really "perfect" Christians—if we would make them real servants of the Saviour—we must get them involved in the saving process, that is, in searching for and finding the lost.

ARN So we're back to the importance of the local church equipping its laity for ministry?

McGAVRAN Yes indeed. But ministry, you know, is a very broad word. We should use a narrower word, a more exact word: Evangelism! If a church is to grow, it must equip its members for evangelism, train them to lead others to Christ. Biblically, you see, every Christian is a witness. We find as we study church growth around the world, that the church grows best when every Christian is trained in, and works at, evangelism. So, while the task of the local church is to equip its laity for "the ministry," if the church would grow, it must equip laymen for this special sort of ministry we're discussing, namely, evangelism.

ARN Let me underscore this principle: evangelism which reaches out helps the church to grow and is effective as laymen are trained and functioning as witnesses.

McGAVRAN We must not kid ourselves into thinking that if we are good Christians in a general sense, and have wonderful fellowship with each other, somehow or other as a result, the church will magically start to grow.

LEADERSHIP QUALITIES

ARN What qualities do you see as essential in leadership for growing churches?

McGAVRAN Let me mention five. First, lay leaders need biblical convictions about man's salvation. They must believe that men are lost without Christ, that God desires all men to be saved, and that the simple God-given way of salvation (repentance and faith in Christ) has been clearly revealed through Christ in the Bible.

The second quality is willingness to give regular time to evangelism. If people are to help churches grow, they must be willing to give freely of their resources, a very important one of which is their time.

The third quality is basic training in evangelism. This is the heart of any program for outreach and growth. We must have regular training sessions for evangelism.

A fourth requirement is that men and women being trained must report regularly to the board or session as to what objectives have been met. The church board session should give regular time to hearing what is being done, what is being planned, and what the outcomes have been —sharing in the defeats and rejoicing in the victories.

The fifth quality I emphasize is prayer. In growing churches you see men and women praying for specific individuals by name—not just that the message may be blessed in general, not that our afternoon's work may prosper, but that Bill and Henry and Mary and Gladys may hear and yield themselves to Christ.

These five I consider essential qualities of leadership. Your experience here in the United States may lead you to emphasize other qualities necessary in lay leaders. How would you answer that question?

ARN I would like to see in leadership positions laymen who can thrust forward the ministry. I would look for a "new breed" of person, a Christian who is *free* to live close to Jesus Christ and *free* to move out into his world. I would also look for laymen who are contagious in their re-productibility, laymen who sense the truth that growth is up to them, and who willingly accept the challenge. They can identify their children in the Lord. They know that evangelism rests on them, not on a meeting somewhere or on their pastor alone. They see themselves as being involved in contagious church growth.

I also see laymen today involved in small groups—mission bands—people who meet together, who pray for one another, who can share their joys and their sorrows and have the kind of supportive personal relationship from which they move out. Finally, these laymen would have the authentic experience of relating to other people. When people hurt, when people need assistance, when people are responsive—laymen are available. They are available in Christian love to point people to the Master and to help them share His faith.

McGAVRAN I'm glad you said that. Those qualities and convictions are an essential part of this matter of training laymen. The characteristics you describe are essential if the church is to grow.

84

THE LAITY

ARN If the church is to grow, all Christians should be mobilized for evangelism.

McGAVRAN Ordinary people have extraordinary abilities. I have great confidence in ordinary Christians: teachers, businessmen, mechanics, typists, housewives, students. What a tremendous number of *contacts* these Christians have.

ARN Have you seen this potential tapped?

McGAVRAN This potential is being tapped at the present time in many places. Let me tell you about one. In the Philippines a movement called "Christ the Only Way" is forming ten thousand Lay Evangelistic Group Studies. The first requirement of each such group is that it be a lay group. The minister seldom attends and is never the leader. All groups are led by laymen. The second requirement is that the group must be evangelistic, not just a meeting of Christians. If more than 50 percent of those attending are Christians, the group is not counted! A third requirement is that the group studies the Bible according to a program tailored to the unchurched. So you have ten thousand Lay Evangelistic Group Studies.

Now these groups are proving to be a great source of converts. These groups are winning non-Christians. In these groups non-Christians feel quite at home because they are in their own neighborhoods and the Christians are their friends. Each visitor is in a small group and non-Christians don't feel intimidated; nobody is accusing them of not going to church. They are just having a good time with their neighbors.

Out of these Lay Evangelistic Group Studies many new churches are arising. This Philippine experiment is a good model, but in whatever way it is done, we must equip Christians in the United States to spread the faith to *millions*. It is not sufficient to bring a few people into our church. The task is to win millions who do not now know Christ to earnest, ardent faith in Him. Nothing else will roll back the tide of materialistic, superficial, sinful living.

THE CLERGY

ARN   Indeed, Christ died for the whole world and if one's desires are anything less, they are not God's desires. But now we've been speaking of laymen and their role in building the church. What about the clergyman? What is his role?

McGAVRAN   The minister in our churches must not do the evangelism by himself. His duty is rather to train other Christians to do it. The minister by himself can do a rather small amount. He should not count on preaching such good sermons that he will pull in non-Christians to hear him. That isn't happening today and doesn't seem likely to happen. The minister must think about his sermon as perfecting those who are already Christians. He should become one who trains Christians to do evangelism. If he does not know how to win men and women, he should learn. The minister's first task is to grow skillful in personal evangelism, then take his people, one by one, and let them learn by doing. The minister teaches evangelism or calls someone in who can teach it. My conviction is that somehow the ministry must lead the laity in evangelizing.

ARN   I had an exciting conversation a few days ago with a minister who had discovered how he can lead his laymen into evangelism. In the past he had taught many courses in evangelism, but the people never evangelized. Now he is using a reproduction method where he takes two laymen with him for a home visit. After these laymen are trained, they train other laymen. The minister is training others, not by telling them how, but by actually *showing* them how.

McGAVRAN   An excellent plan!

ARN   The minister is excited about what's happening not only in the lives of his laymen, but in his own life as well. He is amazed how open people are and that they receive Christ so gladly.

McGAVRAN   Meeting with success such as this moves one from pessimism to optimism, doesn't it?

BEGINNING

ARN   In our conversation about leadership, we must talk about the starting point.

McGAVRAN   You must start where you are, not where you'd like to be. In a given church, perhaps getting started means just a few laymen and their minister. Perhaps a small group which meets regularly for prayer is all that is possible. Each Christian who goes in for evangelism must decide how to start, but whether he starts big or small, he must start. He must find a group of people who will meet regularly to learn about evangelism, to pray about evangelism, and to evangelize!

ARN   Wouldn't it be a marvelous thing if that small group were composed of the leaders of the church? If they could be involved in this kind of outreach, evangelism would permeate the whole structure of the church.

McGAVRAN   Yes, that would be marvelous. Suppose

you got the chairman of the board, the superintendent of the Sunday School, and half a dozen other key people who would covenant together to spend some time each week in study, in sharing their defeats and victories, in sharing their embarrassments as they presented Christ, as well as their joys. What a revolutionary effect it would have on the church!

ARN A group to which all were mutually committed, which held all responsible, would indeed have a revolutionary effect on the church—also on the lives of those in the group.

McGAVRAN Of course, one can start in a much larger way, but whether he starts large or small, he must not just talk about church growth, he must do it.

FATIGUE

ARN That's fine from the professional viewpoint, but can't you hear overworked laymen saying, "Oh, they are adding more weight on my back. I can't do what I am already supposed to do. I'm tired! Frankly, I'm fatigued with church work."

McGAVRAN There are a lot of tired Christians, and it is perfectly true that much of the load of each church is carried by a small number of people. Yet, when you analyze it, you will find that it is *not really tiredness* but *unsuccessfulness* that brings fatigue. If members are trying to induce church growth, but are not successful in bringing people into the church, members tend to feel tired and discouraged. If, on the other hand, their efforts lead others to the Lord and new members to the church, the rewards are tremendous, and rather than feeling tired, they feel exuberant.

ARN   Exuberance and joy accompany success.

McGAVRAN   It goes back to what we've stressed earlier. We need to build up concepts of evangelism, training for evangelism, and leaders for evangelism who really get it done and who experience joy in the process and victory in service.

CLASSES OF LEADERS

ARN   As we discuss leadership for growing churches, let's talk about the several kinds of leaders.

McGAVRAN   I think you mean the five classes of leaders which growing churches need. I call them Class One, Class Two, Class Three, Class Four and Class Five leaders. You must not call these first class, second class, or third class leaders. None of them are third class leaders! You must use the right terminology. Class One, Class Two, Class Three, Class Four and Class Five. Yes, this concept has been found quite useful.

ARN   What do these classes represent? What are the distinctions?

McGAVRAN   Class One leaders are those who serve the existing church. They're Sunday School teachers, deacons, elders, choir members, ushers, ladies who arrange flowers, and those who phone or visit members who are sick—that great army of able Christians who contribute time so liberally and to such good effect in our churches. What a poor place the church would be without Class One leaders!

ARN   Class One, by the large, carries on the maintenance ministry of the church. What about Class Two?

McGAVRAN Class Two leaders are volunteer workers who head out away from the church. They actively reach out to others in the community who need Christ. You see them going two by two down the street ringing doorbells, or inviting people to a home Bible study, or doing any one of a number of things that help people come to a knowledge of Jesus Christ.

I was touring through the Philippines by bus, when the pastor accompanying me pointed out the window to four or five young people scrambling up a little narrow path through a bamboo grove. "See those young people?"

I said, "Yes, I see them. What about them?"

He replied, "They are going five miles—over that hill and down the other side to a village to hold a church service with three Christian families. Because they sing well, they'll attract quite a number of the non-Christians." That's an example of Class Two leaders.

ARN So Class Two leaders are those involved in any form of outreach to non-Christians.

McGAVRAN Yes, and their numbers should be very great. Now, Class Threes are leaders of small churches.

ARN They might be partially paid . . .

McGAVRAN Or they may be completely unpaid. They could lead a house church of four or five families that assemble regularly.

ARN These leaders would be working with small groups of Christians helping them get established.

McGAVRAN Small assemblies of Christians are a very important part of church growth. Normally, each church as it begins to grow is rather a small group. We tend to feel

Classes of Leaders

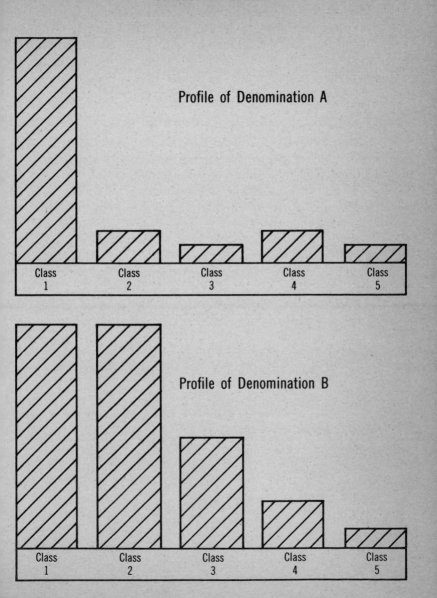

Profile of Denomination A

Class 1 Class 2 Class 3 Class 4 Class 5

Profile of Denomination B

Class 1 Class 2 Class 3 Class 4 Class 5

that the only way to start a church is to have a big, beautifully appointed building. If that is true, we're not going to start many new churches. The churches that meet in small, unimpressive places are important, and their leaders are Class Three leaders. We need thousands of them!

Class Four leaders are the paid, professional leaders of large, well-established congregations. They are important. Class Five leaders travel from one country to another, know two or three languages, and are part of the world church.

ARN In America, Class Fives would be the denominational leaders or district leaders.

McGAVRAN Yes, the leadership beyond the local or state level.

ARN Before us are five classes of leaders. If your desire were to see your church grow, how would you distribute the leadership available to you into the Five Classes?

McGAVRAN A most important question. The proportion of leaders in each class is a matter of great significance. On the accompanying page, readers will see a diagram of two denominations, Denomination A and Denomination B. Observe the profile of each, and you will discover that Denomination A has a large number of Class One leaders, practially no Class Two leaders, and few Class Three leaders. Denomination A has a fair number of Class Fours and Class Fives. This is a typical American denomination.

Now look at Denomination B. It has a good number of Class One leaders, the unpaid volunteer leaders serving the existing church. But look; it has more Class Two leaders who are working in outreach than it has Class Ones! It also has a good number of Class Threes, leaders of small

Growth in Different Classes of Leaders in Denomination A

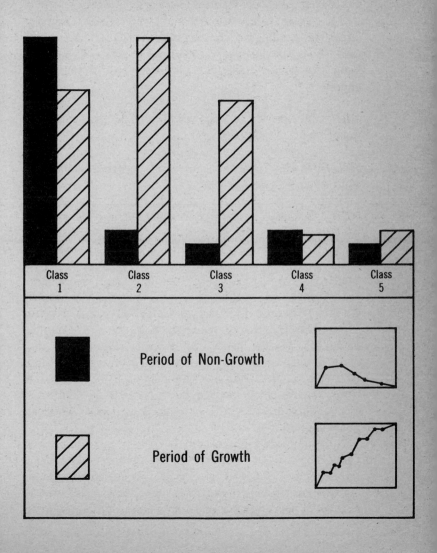

churches or Christian cells or Bible studies in the home, call them what you will. Then it has a rather small number of Class Four leaders, and an even smaller number of Class Five leaders. As you look at that diagram, which denomination do you suppose is growing now and has potential for future growth?

ARN I see direct relationship between growth and many Class Two and Class Three leaders. "B" is growing. "A" is not.

McGAVRAN You are quite correct. Denomination B is the one which is growing. Denomination A will not grow, because no one is working towards growth. If Denomination A wants to grow, it must find ways to increase Class Two and Class Three leaders.

ARN Can we move beyond a denominational growth pattern to the local church? I see this same principle applying there. In the use of leadership, a church must strategize and deploy leadership for growth.

McGAVRAN Every local church would be well advised to count the number of its Class One, Class Two, and Class Three leaders. Such a study would be revealing. Most churches would probably find an over-abundance of Class One leaders. If a church wants to grow, its goal should be an equal number of Class Ones and Class Twos.

ARN While these classes of leadership are most helpful, I can see how these divisions are not airtight. They are interrelated and overlap in many ways.

McGAVRAN Oh, yes. Class One leaders are usually wonderful Christians. If you train them and turn them loose, they make very good Class Two leaders. We should not imagine that some people become Class Ones and are sealed off to that, while others become Class Two and are sealed to that. There not only is, but there should be, much overlapping.

ARN The Sunday School teacher in the classroom is Class One; but as that same teacher does personal evangelism (and possibly builds the class while doing so) he or she becomes a Class Two leader.

McGAVRAN Yes, and he'll be a better teacher of the Bible if he is winning people to Christ. The Bible will come alive for him and he'll find new depths of meaning. He'll communicate essential Christianity better to his students if he is showing them by example how to introduce men to eternal life.

ARN In concluding this chapter on leadership for growing churches, can you give us one illustration of the principle we've been discussing?

McGAVRAN There's a rapidly growing church in the great city of San Juan in Puerto Rico. This was a resistant city. There had been little Protestant church growth there. In fact, it was a city where churches died. On Pearl Harbor day in 1941, a church was organized in a home, with nine members. Thirteen years later, it had grown to 627 members, a notable case of church growth.

"How did it happen?" I asked Rev. Isidro Diaz, the pastor. "You must preach very powerful sermons."

He replied, "My sermons have little to do with it. You see we have twelve upper rooms."

"What do you mean?" I asked.

"We have divided our congregation into twelve sections, and each conducts a full worship service, except for the Communion, every week," he said.

95

I replied, "That must keep you busy running from one service to another."

He said, "I never attend any of them. That's not my business. That's the business of the laymen."

"Oh," I said, "so you have twelve branch churches, then, led by laymen?"

He replied, "Yes! That is where the unchurched first start coming to worship. They wouldn't think of coming to the church. That's too formidable, but to a neighborhood meeting they go quite readily. These twelve house churches, each with about fifty members, give us an opportunity to grow."

That illustration is replete with lessons on church growth. Observe that, instead of one church having a relatively few people carrying the real responsibility, you now have 12 churches. In each one at least six people carry the responsibility. So you have 70 or 80 taking an active part in, and feeling the responsibility of, church growth. Each of the 12 congregations is engaged in evangelizing its neighbors. Visitors become part of a small church, small enough so real friendship can be developed, real care can be exercised, and real koinonia can be experienced. Real responsibility is delegated to laymen. They run these 12 churches, all by themselves!

The night I spoke at that church in Puerto Rico, a high school teacher confessed Christ. She had attended one of these upper rooms for over a year. After becoming a believer, she came to the main church to formally confess Christ, where later she was baptized and received her first Communion. Following this, she continued as a member of the upper room (house church) in which she had found the Lord.

ARN The principle, then, is that for church growth to occur, recruiting and training lay leaders is necessary—leaders who function as Class Twos and Class Threes. In any growing church, you will find this principle in action as enthusiastic, trained laymen carry on the work of Christ and His Church.

CHAPTER 6

Characteristics of Growing Churches

ARN A study of growing churches indicates that some characteristics in them appear again and again. These do not appear with the same intensity in all situations, yet to some degree each plays a prominent role in growing churches. In this chapter we are not endeavoring to deal in depth with any of these characteristics, but rather to open each for further analysis and discussion.

GROWTH GOALS

McGAVRAN Growth goals indicate that the church takes its work seriously. It thinks through its mission and formulates goals with great care. It discusses these goals for weeks or months before stating them. In the process the church is bound into a certain unity. A decision is not made unless the members of the board, the members of the church, the minister, the various people concerned, are all agreed.

Incidentally, discussions on church growth such as we are having might be the first stage in the formation of growth goals. It would be a great pity for any group to work through this book and then not set growth goals for its church. After the readers have thought about their church from all these various points of view, it would be natural for them to say, "Under our circumstances, the will of God for us is that we do so and so."

ARN It is interesting to note that if a church does not have any goals, individual organizations and individual Christians in the church will have their own, though often unstated, goals. The choir pursues its goals, the youth group works toward its goals, the women seek their goals, and the church is pulled in many different directions. Because these forces are pulling different ways, the total church does not move forward. The opposite condition prevails when there is a unity of goals in which all of the various individuals and groups participate. Then all the parts of the church head in the same direction, and it moves forward. It grows!

McGAVRAN A church drifts like an unanchored boat unless it has definite growth goals! An essential part of growth goals is that each member of the church should feel that he has had a share in making them. They should not be imposed from the outside, but should grow up from within, based on the conviction of the members, so they can say, "These are our goals."

ARN It appears that the more Christians can pray and talk their goals through, the more they will "own" them. When unity and agreement are reached, more people will work toward goal accomplishment.

McGAVRAN Yes, and goals should be both short-range and long-range. If the goal, for example, is that a church double its numbers or plant several daughter churches, that may very well be the long-range goal. The first short-range goal may be to conduct classes so every-body in the church gets well-grounded in the biblical nec-essity for church growth and sees the need which every man has for Jesus Christ.

ARN It is often a good plan to break down the long-range goals into smaller sub-goals (units); for example, a five-year goal might be broken down into yearly goals, then broken down again into monthly segments. With such a division, progress is easily seen.

UTILIZES TIME

ARN Let me illustrate by sharing with you a film, "Charlie Churchman," that I produced some years ago. In it we satirized a board meeting. This satire showed people coming late, inadequate preparation, an agenda dealing with superficialities, all of which went on and on and on.

McGAVRAN That sounds painfully familiar.

ARN We photographed the old clock on the wall. We used a cobweb machine and blew gossamers over Charlie and the other board members. The viewers laugh. It is a funny sequence, but the reason they laugh is that there is truth in it. Haven't we all lived through board meetings that seemed to be eternal?

McGAVRAN A growing church treats meetings of the church as if they were matters of real importance. That means preparation so that the necessary information is on hand and decisions can be made.

ARN So often our church work is carried on in a sloppy, unprepared manner. Churches that are growing utilize time and make meetings count.

McGAVRAN I think that is true. They know where they are going and intend to get there. They feel commissioned by God to do a certain task. A sense of urgency and of importance marks growing churches.

ARN Importance and urgency are good words and are also seen in action in all meetings of the church; for example, in a growing church one doesn't find a song leader having people sing five or six hymns "to fill out the hour." There is urgency. There is purpose. Something happens when people gather.

McGAVRAN Christians would generally agree that the business of the church should be conducted with even greater care and attention than the secular enterprises they are involved in throughout the week. The gatherings of God's people should be marked by good planning and prompt execution.

ARN How people feel about a meeting is very important, sometimes even more important than the content of a meeting.

McGAVRAN I agree. If people feel their time is being well spent, that they are not wasting it, you have a weighty moral factor on your side.

ARN We can summarize by saying that a growing church "redeems the time."

MEMBERS COMMITTED TO DISCIPLESHIP

McGAVRAN Committed is the key word in that heading. Members are committed to Christ not only in general, but to Christ's specific purpose—to bring men and women to believe on Himself and thus to find eternal life.

102

ARN True discipleship means that the disciple has the same goals and objectives as his Master. But being committed to discipleship has an additional dimension in growing churches. Discipleship suggests active involvement.

McGAVRAN Right! Christians are working at winning others to Christ. They look at the community round about them and see men and women who really ought to know Jesus. They bring in reports as to the numbers who have received Christ. They have plans for growth. In other words, they are committed to winning others.

ARN When Jesus called His disciples, He said, "Follow me and I will make you to become fishers of men." (See Mark 1:17.) That is still the call of discipleship today.

SMALL GROUP FELLOWSHIP

ARN William James suggests that the basis for effective organized movements is small groups of committed people. Small groups are the purifying element of the church. They are the praying element of the church. They are the dynamic. The church needs small groups as the loaf needs the yeast. In small groups there can be strength, power and outreach to change and move the church—to change and move the community and the world.

McGAVRAN In some cases, small groups would have to be created. In other cases, the existing church structure could be revamped.

ARN A church would have to survey its membership and determine if all are involved in small groups where Christians can be served and where they in turn can serve others. To meet this need some churches have altered their structure; others have totally restructured.

103

McGAVRAN   Dr. Meyers is the authority for the statement that if you want a Sunday School to grow, you must break down every class of more than twelve. Whenever a class gets to be twelve or more, divide it and start a new class. He believes that only small groups come to know each other well enough to have the dynamics described.

ARN   Today as one observes the characteristics of growing churches, small groups are most significant.

McGAVRAN   Dr. Meyers' study indicated that the growth of a church did not correlate with the training of the minister, or the excellence of the Sunday School, the building, or the musical program. It correlated with the number of small face-to-face groups. If a church had a large number of small face-to-face groups, it grew. If it had big Sunday School classes and big church services, the chances were it did not grow.

I would add that the small-group fellowship must be an evangelistic fellowship. Merely organizing small groups which have a warm spiritual time among themselves does not create growing churches. But if these groups are outward oriented, if they are concerned with the unchurched, if they win other members in the community where they live—in short, if they are evangelistic fellowships, then small groups are very important.

In the Philippines today, small groups are being stressed. Every small group aims to have at least 50 percent of its members consist of those who do not yet know or believe in Jesus Christ. In this way the small groups are made up of Christians and non-Christians in about equal proportions and are very effective in evangelism.

ARN   You're saying that in small groups, while people may enjoy excellent relationships one with another, to be evangelistically effective they must turn outward.

McGAVRAN   They must bring the unchurched into the group. The "yet to believe" must find real fellowship in the group. There is power in small groups if properly used.

UTILIZES DIRECT EVANGELISM

ARN   Across the nation today there are many different models of evangelism. Do you see any successful pattern?

McGAVRAN   Models which have come to the attention of the nation's churches are those which have been successful in at least one church. Other churches can frequently use the same methods—modifying them to meet local circumstances. The important thing is to use them so men and women are in fact led to accept the Saviour.

ARN   Models help us see how others are evangelizing. Remembering that each church has its particular personality and each community has its particular needs, a church is more successful if it can create its own program of direct evangelism which suits itself and its community.

McGAVRAN   In talking and planning about direct evangelism, let's be honest and list the direct evangelism that we are really doing and the amount of time we're really putting into it. Sometimes we'll find we are doing a good deal. Often we'll find that we are doing very little. Our need is to begin to do something, to innovate, or borrow, or adapt. In most cases, Christians should greatly increase the amount of direct evangelism they are doing.

ARN   There is a relationship between the amount of time and effort and the number of people involved in direct evangelism and the growth of the church.

McGAVRAN   No question about it. The number of people working at it has a great deal to do with the outcome. If, in Church One, you have twenty people working in direct evangelism, and in Church Two you have 200, Church Two will grow more than Church One.

ARN Considering direct evangelism, I would like to emphasize that we're not talking of a special crusade once every four years lasting a week or two, or of a once-a-year evangelistic emphasis in a local church. We're calling for a consistent program of evangelism fifty-two weeks of the year.

McGAVRAN This is absolutely true. Churches that have an evangelistic week once a year are not, as a rule, growing churches but those that have regular evangelistic work going on all the time, with reports at every board meeting, and charts in the pastor's study or the board room showing the growth of the church—these are the churches which are growing.

MULTIPLE MINISTRY TO MEET PEOPLE'S NEEDS

ARN People are different. They don't fit one mold. A church that recognizes these individual differences and strives to meet people's needs, tends to grow.

McGAVRAN That's right. We've been speaking a lot about evangelism, but evangelism must not be interpreted in a narrow sense. Evangelism is not simply button-holing people and speaking to them about Jesus; there must be a concern for their needs. The church must be willing and ready to meet people where they are.

For example, if families with young children begin to attend the church, adequate nursery facilities must be provided so that the mothers can come to church and worship

106

while their youngsters are being cared for. Possibly a scout troop or recreation for the young people should be organized. Perhaps classes in English would help some members of minority communities. True evangelism loves *persons,* recognizes their needs and tries to help them.

But remember, meeting needs, by itself, is not evangelism. Social action must not be substituted for evangelism. Sheep must be found, brought to the fold, and fed.

ARN A growing church, then, is a church sensitive to the needs of its own people, to the needs of the community, to the needs of the world, and endeavors to meet these needs on many different fronts. But I can see danger in getting too broad.

McGAVRAN Many churches multiply good deeds while not growing at all. This is why it is very necessary to have a church growth conscience. Christians should be not primarily serving men's *temporal* needs. We serve them because they are children of God. We serve them because they are immortal souls and have eternal needs. We meet their temporal needs at a dozen different places. But we should beware lest we simply wait on tables, or simply heal bodies. Christians must regard others as bodies *and souls,* and strive to meet the needs of "the whole man who is made in the image of *God.*"

ARN A church which meets the needs of the whole man is a growing church. It grows because all people have needs and will respond to such a church.

TRAINS LEADERS

ARN I believe that leadership training, from the New Testament church until today, has been a chief secret of growing churches.

McGAVRAN That's right, but it must be leadership training of a particular sort. Leadership training comes in fifty assorted colors. You can train leaders in many ways. We must make sure that leaders are trained in church growth. They must come to have "church-growth eyes." They must see the congregation as a *church* not a Christian club. They must see the city as in great need of Jesus Christ and the church as the answer to that need. In short, all of us must think about leadership training from a thoroughly Christian perspective.

ARN Leadership development presupposes a plan whereby training in church growth is carried on continually.

McGAVRAN I'd like to suggest that every church can institute regular training classes in church growth. With the educated membership of the American church, and the abundant books and magazines available, any group can study church growth and see how it bears upon its particular community.

ARN Contemporary church growth can be an exciting study. For example, a church shouldn't simply say, "We are a church in Houston or Columbus or Milwaukee," but "We are a church in a particular part of our city and our particular neighborhood has certain characteristics. Our church will grow in certain ways and it will not grow in other ways. The people who need Christ in this segment of the city are different from the people who need Christ in another segment of the city."

McGAVRAN That kind of thinking can become, and ought to become, commonplace to the whole membership —men, women, and youth. Creating that kind of thinking is what I mean by "training leaders for church growth."

108

ARN When Jesus sent out the 70 two by two, apparently this outreach was preceded by training.

McGAVRAN Yes! He told them they were to announce that the Kingdom of God was at hand. In the preceding days, our Lord had been telling them what the Kingdom of God means. When they went to those villages in the high country of Judea, the 70 taught what they had learned about the Kingdom of God. Part of the amazing growth of the church after the Lord's resurrection was, no doubt, due to this evangelistic tour and to the training He had given His disciples before sending them out.

ARN We've been considering characteristics of growing churches. Now our readers should take the important step of discussing these characteristics and applying them to their own particular congregations and communities.

CHAPTER 7

"First Church"

ARN Let's look at a profile of "First Church." Although every church is unique, they do fall into types. The church I'm about to describe is a typical downtown church. Its spire points heavenward among the buildings of the business district. Commercial structures encircle it.

The membership is numbered in the thousands, many of whom are inactive. Members live in outlying areas and commute to the services. At "First Church" large family groupings pride themselves on having been members for three generations. Many rooms and facilities of the church have family names connected with them. Loyalty to the church has slackened with each generation; however, endowments and gifts continue family traditions. Membership in "First Church" is associated with leadership in the community. Prestigious people make this their home church.

The congregation consists of many older adults, some middle-aged adults, and a few young adults. The Sunday

School and youth programs attract some from the neighboring community whose parents do not attend the church. The growth curve that once climbed upward, plateaued some years ago, and recently has been declining.

The architecture is in the style of a few generations ago. The facilities exceed the present needs of the congregation and provide abundant space for sports, worship services, Christian education, fellowship and banquets.

Because of endowments and all-member canvasses, financing the church is not a problem. Church income meets the needs of the local church, the denomination, and other causes. The wealth of the church is reflected in its multiple ministries. A large staff is employed. The payroll includes twenty-three employees. Laymen delegate to the specialized staff all the work of the church. Some lay involvement is seen in boards, committees and other functions, but primarily the congregation looks to the paid staff to do what it is paid for!!

The worship service is the focal point of "First Church," and much emphasis is placed on the pulpit message.

McGAVRAN You have described a common congregation. Each city has several, and across the nation there are many thousands. "First Church" has had an honorable history. In fact, it has been one of the leading churches in its denomination, and at the present time it's carrying on a notable service ministry. The twenty-three employed staff members are doing a great deal of very good work.

SICKNESS SYMPTOMS

ARN As you look at this church, do you feel it is healthy?

McGAVRAN No, I do not. Despite the fact that it has

112

*". . . there stands a non-reproductive
church, a static church, a sterile church,
and this is not normal. It's sick!"*

an honorable history and is doing notable present service,
from the point of view of reproductiveness, this church is
sick. Membership is declining. Yet "First Church" might
very well have brought into its folds literally thousands of
the unchurched, spiritually hungry, frustrated and alienat-
ed people that surge around the church. In other words, in
the midst of multitudes who need Christ, there stands a
non-reproductive church, a static church, a sterile church,
and this is not normal. It's sick!

ARN Sick? What are some of the symptoms of the disease?

McGAVRAN One prominent symptom is what I call
clerical dominance. "First Church" is run by its paid staff.
Mind you, the laymen play a part. They are on the board.
They play leading parts perhaps in some of the domestic
concerns of the church. Nevertheless, this church with its
twenty-three paid staff members, its fine sermons, its beau-

113

tiful music, its worship service of outstanding quality is dominated by its clergy.

ARN Thousands of churches across the nation are earnestly struggling to increase the size of their staff. You are saying this is not the ideal.

McGAVRAN This is exactly what I'm saying. A book by Neil Braun illustrates my point. He studied the churches around the world in terms of the proportion of paid staff to the membership of the church and found that usually when the number of paid staff is high, a non-growing church results. But where lay leadership is heavily emphasized, there is a growing church. His book is called *Laity Mobilized* and while it describes conditions abroad, it would be well worth reading all across America.

ARN Do I understand what you're saying—that a paid staff is a good thing, but not when it takes over responsibility which belongs to laymen?

McGAVRAN Yes. Paid leaders must say to themselves, "It is not primarily what *we do,* it is primarily what we get *others to do* that counts."

ARN Now apply that to "First Church."

McGAVRAN I am not saying, "Fire the paid staff!" but rather, "Let the staff train the entire membership in church growth." Suppose we assume the membership of this church to be 2300 with a paid staff of 23. To every member of the staff you would say, "Learn how to win others to Christ and organize them into Christian cells. Then take your 100 of the 2300 and train them in personal evangelism." Immediately that church would be operating on a different wave length.

114

ARN As we look at "First Church," are there other symptoms of sickness?

McGAVRAN Yes, a related problem of "First Church" is that all the laymen who are working in the church are Class One leaders. In other words, their concern is solely with the maintenance of the church. They are benefiting existing members. They are on the building committee, the youth committee, the Sunday School staff, the board, or the board of trustees—all concerned, but all Class One leaders. There are not enough Class Twos or Class Threes. Of the 2300 members in this church, you would find few engaged in any kind of evangelism. This imbalance should be corrected.

ARN A church that has primarily Class One leaders is self-centered and bound to no growth.

SMALL GROUPS

McGAVRAN Exactly! Indeed, one can say that growth is practically impossible. Therefore, one of the things this church needs to do is to establish scores of outward-looking small groups. You've seen small groups revolutionize the life of a church. Could you describe the process as it might operate in "First Church"?

ARN Small groups would be important in "First Church." The 2300 members need to form many responsible groups both for their own growth and for the growth of the church. They need to relate. They need to identify. They need to really know one another so members are not lost in the bigness of it all. The small group has other functions as well; it should train its members.

You spoke earlier of each minister training a hundred people. I see each hundred being broken down into smaller groups in which each paid staff member would personally train several key leaders who would, in turn, train others. In this way there would soon be a multiplying number of Class Two leaders, and a new spirit of relationship would penetrate the entire church.

McGAVRAN It is necessary to remember that small groups can become introverted. If small groups of existing Christians meet together, study the Bible together, pray together, get to know each other, feel kindly toward one another, and the process stops there, you haven't gained much. You've gained only a good feeling among the saints. That's good, but we must have more than that. Every small group must be open-ended *toward the world*. Every small group must say to itself, "We have failed unless, and until, in this small group we have converted some of the unconverted, and fed some of the spiritually hungry."

RESISTANCE TO CHANGE

ARN This brings us back to an earlier principle of church growth—"seeing the possibilities." Think how easy it is for members of "First Church" to have non-growth excuses: "We like it like it is." "Why should we grow?" "We're as big as we want to be." All these excuses for non-growth must be swept away, and the vision and the burden we find throughout the New Testament must characterize all organizations and members of the church.

McGAVRAN Every church works out a rationalization and a defense for itself. Sometimes the very minister of the church will work out a theological defense for things as they are. He will not only say, "We like it this way," but will say, "God wants it this way." He will quote Scripture that it should be this way, that this is what is called for by God. If a church is long on quality and short on quantity,

116

he points out that God is interested in quality and not in quantity. These rationalizations are very seductive. Christians must be on their guard against them. Ministers in particular must be sure that they are not devising theological arguments which are really rationalizations of defeat.

GROWTH GOALS

ARN We say that growing churches have growth goals. Do you see these goals in "First Church"?

McGAVRAN No, that's prime reason for its failure to grow. There's no rock-ribbed intention to plant daughter churches, to win other people to Christ, to raise a family, so to speak. This church continues to watch a declining membership with contentment or resignation. They may not like it, but they don't know quite what to do about it. Their kind of people have moved out to the suburbs, and those who now live within a mile or two of the church aren't coming. Even if the neighbors do visit the church, they don't feel comfortable. There's this whole matter of different sub-cultures that we discussed previously. This church's members are of one American sub-culture. Those round about the church are of another. Consequently, effective evangelism will take more than good intentions, more than spontaneous effort of one sort or another. It is going to take hard, bold plans. It is going to take positive determination to grow. "First Church" must see the real situation and do an about-face in its basic policies.

ARN From what we know about "First Church," then, what specific goals could you envision for them?

McGAVRAN The first thing in the development of church-growth goals is a survey of possibilities. What growth possibilities does "First Church" really have?

ARN   A survey of possibilities both within the community and in the church, to find homogeneous groups in which viable Christian cells can be started.

McGAVRAN   This church plans to locate, say, half a dozen places where there are real church-growth opportunities. Now any adequate survey will reveal not half a dozen, but many more opportunities. The survey should go on until two dozen opportunities are arrayed before the church board, the staff, and the members. The survey may cost ten thousand dollars, but money is one thing "First Church" has.

ARN   With the array of possibilities revealed, the next step is to determine priorities. Which opportunities hold the greatest promise? In what order should they be developed?

McGAVRAN   Then intelligent plans need to be drawn to mine these veins of ore; for example, "First Church" could plant churches in suitable populations miles away, or it could determine to multiply cells in its immediate neighborhood. At this point, the minister and laymen may need the services of a church-growth consultant, one with expertise in this area.

ARN   Briefly summarizing, "First Church" does, indeed, need growth goals. These will be formed as the community, along with the church, is surveyed, and factual information becomes available. In the community are homogeneous groupings which will be compatible and "First Church" will conclude, "This should be an area of concentration." As opportunities are seen, priorities should be carefully established and resources assembled to develop these growth possibilities.

*"A large part of the problem here
is that growth studies at various levels have
not been done . . . a simple line graph. . . ."*

MEASURING

ARN What's next?

McGAVRAN Part of the process of waking "First Church" to the opportunities for church growth and of creating a conscience on the matter is to measure the existing growth of the church. A large part of the problem here is that growth studies at various levels have not been done. I imagine that a simple line graph of the growth of this church over the last thirty years would be instructive to every member of the congregation. Furthermore, if line graphs were drawn according to age levels, the process would be even more revealing. What about the growth of the membership of the "fifty and over" graph? How much growth has there been of the young adult group? What about growth of the youth? What percentage of the membership comes from the suburbs? How many come from the immediate vicinity? If studies such as these were done,

119

members would know exactly the rate at which the church and its constituent parts are, or are not, growing. When this survey has been completed and the findings have been shared with the members, "First Church" will be in a very much better position to plan for growth.

ARN You mentioned *members* knowing these facts. I believe that is an important concept. Often leaders, lay or clergy, have this information, but so often it is not widely known to the congregation. Effective communication in a church of any size is most important, and the larger the group, the more difficult the problem.

McGAVRAN Suppose every member of the church had exact knowledge as to the past history of growth, the growth possibilities and plans for growth. Suppose that measurement were to reveal that while this church was doing a lot of good work—philanthropy, boys' and girls' clubs, basketball, etc.—none of these activities resulted in communicating the faith. Instead of "First Church" having literally hundreds of converts and a dozen branches scattered round, suppose it was found to be doing many good works and slowly withering away!!

ARN How threatening for a pastor to have to reveal to his people that the church is not progressing. In fact, it's threatening to anyone to reveal the "other" side.

McGAVRAN We've got to quantify what's happening in terms of the growth of the church so that it can be seen. The quality of "First Church" may be high; that's not where it is sick; it's sick in quantity. One of the things that must be done to regain health and vigor is for "First Church" from top to bottom to gain a conscience on its duty to communicate the Christian faith to others in its city.

120

LEADERSHIP DEVELOPMENT

ARN A characteristic of a growing church is that it trains leaders. In the profile of "First Church," we find that leadership is exercised by older adults. Now, how do you view this?

McGAVRAN As a normal and reasonable sort of thing. Who are the leaders? They're responsible older members. They're the tried and tested people who, when they say they'll be there, actually arrive! Leadership gravitates to dependable people. But when it does, you are left with a group of older members, and the new converts, the new additions to the church, don't get much chance to lead. The new converts are few to begin with and are not pushed into leadership. In order to grow, therefore, we must measure lay leadership in terms of new convert leaders carrying on man-sized tasks.

ARN It would be embarrassing to find there are no new converts. This brings to focus the need for evangelistic outreach.

McGAVRAN As evangelistic outreach takes place, some new converts will be won. These new converts must, to the highest degree possible, be set to doing something in which they can have a responsible and honorable part. They may not be doing some things the older members have been doing, but it is important to lead new members into Christian activities they can do.

ARN So, if "First Church" is going to grow, it must have a flexibility in organization and structure which allows new converts to work.

McGAVRAN Exactly!

REPRODUCTION

ARN "First Church" has done well in giving to the central denominational funds and to missions.

McGAVRAN Giving is a good thing to do but not entirely adequate. I suppose "First Church" is one of the heaviest giving churches in the denomination. Whenever the secretary of the Missionary Society is in this part of the country, he comes to "First Church" and speaks. Members are proud of their "missionary record," which for the most part consists of their giving to the denomination. How the money is spent, the members are not sure. Furthermore, were they to make an investigation, they would find that a great deal of their money goes into social service or into social action: hospitals, leprosy homes, literacy work and other institutional approaches.

ARN What is your point?

McGAVRAN My point is that all these are good works, but how much giving is going into propagating the Christian faith?

ARN You believe that overseas, as well as in America, a church must spend a good deal of its resources in propagating the Christian Faith?

McGAVRAN Yes! "First Church" ought to have the assurance that its giving will reproduce Christian churches overseas. Giving money for philanthropy overseas only reproduces the same kind of conscience here. Do you see how the same pattern is followed? "First Church" does good in its neighborhood, and whether anyone comes to Christ or not, overseas or at home, is a matter of secondary importance. If leaders in "First Church" can encourage and implant a conscience that the Christian faith be multiplied overseas, that Jesus Christ be known and loved and obeyed and followed overseas, then they are also likely to insist that Christ be known here in this neighborhood. When that kind of conscience is created, "First Church" breaks out of its lack of growth pattern into victorious growth overseas and at home.

TOWARD VITALITY ...

ARN   As we've been discussing "First Church," we've decided that her sickness can be cured. This church can bloom in health and growth and vigor.

McGAVRAN   We've focused not so much on the sickness as on the steps which lead to full, radiant health. It's normal for a church to be healthy; if this church with its fine record, its notable history, and its basic Christian dedication, applies church-growth principles, it can lose that extra fifty pounds it is carrying, firm up its muscles and recover abounding health.

ARN   And our discussion of possible steps is really just the beginning.

McGAVRAN   Some suggestions will be more applicable in one church, less applicable in others. Indeed, many other steps might be mentioned and I anticipate that the leaders in this church will come up with many ideas and innovations of their own.

ARN   The end result of thinking together about "First Church" should be growth, vitality, obedience to God and a significant surge forward.

McGAVRAN   No question! There's plenty of opportunity. "First Church" faces the most winnable population on earth. America has never seen greater numbers of winnable persons. And "First Church" never had greater resources with which to win them.

CHAPTER 8

"New Church"

ARN Here's a church which will sound familiar to you. Fifteen people were present for the organizational meeting of "New Church" six months ago. Today twenty-five gather for worship.

The opportunity for planting a church was seen by a few Christian families who had moved into a new and growing community. Those involved in this venture of faith had the blessing and prayer support of their former congregation.

A visitor to "New Church" immediately senses the enthusiasm and purpose which unite the small fellowship. A spirit of pioneering brings life and vitality to the group. Members share the excitement of evangelism. Victories and problems are known to all in the group. The "highs" and "lows" of this new work are more pronounced than members remember in their former churches.

Those in the fellowship are committed to this new enterprise and experience satisfaction in obedience to Christ.

An honest relationship of communication, sharing and purpose exists among members of the group. They depend on the Spirit of God for direction and guidance.

Worship services are held in the biggest room of a rented building. This facility is supplemented by an adjoining home when additional facilities are needed.

Laymen lead in all activities but are searching for a part-time pastor. The church sees its major problems to be facilities, pastoral leadership, and insufficient money to fund the goals of the congregation.

The future seems bright for "New Church." Although the members recognize that pioneering is not without its hardships, they are prepared to endure these.

BIG CHURCHES FROM LITTLE CHURCHES GROW

McGAVRAN "New Church" is a very common type of church. In fact, as you look at the Church exploding and growing all around the world in country after country, you find multitudes of small churches. Just as full-grown men have all been little babies, so full-grown churches all began as little churches. The normal thing for Christians everywhere is to form new churches. They will be small; they will struggle, but remarkably few of them die.

ARN Looking at "New Church," I'm impressed with the opportunity its members face. They're beginning from scratch, and the opportunity is great to establish their church on sound church-growth principles. I get excited about "New Church." Now they can start keeping records that will give them the information necessary to determine how and where they're growing. These records will help them to see their community and to locate the homogeneous groups. I also see opportunity to train the leadership

". . . so full-grown churches all begin as little churches."

for continuous normal evangelism. "New Church" has great opportunities to grow and mature in Christ.

McGAVRAN I'm sure you're right. Each new church gives a number of Christians great opportunities for leadership, creativity, courageous new action and innovations of all sorts. Christians in new churches are doing many things right by using good common sense. However, I agree when you say that if such churches studied church growth, they would do even better. The small congregation and its leaders will inevitably be interested in growth. They realize it is their very lifeblood. They are in a new community where neighbors are in urgent need of Christ and the church. Leaders and members of small churches can study church growth with great interest and with great benefit.

ARN You mentioned creativity. I find this characteristic of great importance in growing churches. Creativity should be encouraged and can be a large asset. "New Church" doesn't have to do exactly as the "Mother Church" does. It doesn't have to hear the excuse, "We've always done it that way before." It discovers new ways to reach people. It can meet needs in unique ways. It is using new wine skins.

PROPER MOTIVES

ARN   "New Church" makes me feel as if I'm reading the New Testament.

McGAVRAN   I hope "New Church" shares New Testament convictions. One of the greatest dangers we face in church growth is that people seek growth for secular motives. This cheapens the whole process. "New Church" must not say, "We want to grow so that we'll be bigger than the Lutherans next door or as big as the Baptists down the street, or even so we'll have more members in order to pay our bills." We do have to pay our bills, but we don't get new members just in order to do that.

We seek new members because the people out there, without Christ, are living poor and starved lives, even if they're prospering financially and drive good cars, even if superficially they appear prosperous. The Christian believes that until a person knows Jesus Christ, until he has the joy of sins forgiven, until he is really a follower of Christ and has a personal experience with Him, he is missing the greatest thing in life. This conviction leads us to speak to others, to win them to Christ, to incorporate them into the church, to give them responsibilities, to train them as leaders, and to send them out in turn to win others. We need much Bible study along this line so that our entire church-growth effort will be done for Christian motives and in obedience to God rather than as a restless search for success.

128

ARN   In the book of the Revelation, when John wrote to the members of the church in Ephesus, he complimented them for doing many things well, but indicted them for leaving their first love. John could have been speaking of this very thing—proper motives.

McGAVRAN   He was speaking about this very thing. We do things that are institutionally correct, that are smooth, that are beautiful, that are polished professionally, and yet the knowledge of the Lord Jesus has somehow escaped, and our first love is gone. "New Church" must be especially careful to be a New Testament church.

The New Testament churches, you know, seem to have had little consciousness of the need to grow. The New Testament records few exhortations to go out and win others to Christ, but Christians did it just the same. They loved the Lord so much they naturally told others about Him.

ARN   Aren't you contradicting yourself? You have been talking about church growth and growth principles. Now you're saying the New Testament churches didn't seem to emphasize growth. Explain that.

McGAVRAN   The answer is fairly simple. If we really have the love of Christ, He will lead us out in many different ways. I assume that most of the Christians reading this book are good Christians. They love the Lord. They have high motivations. All that we have discussed together is intended to lead readers into more fruitful ways of evangelism. I am merely saying, "Look, don't use these principles mechanically. Don't depend solely on them. First, comes love of Christ! Second, comes the ways in which that love will express itself and seek the welfare of others."

ARN "Love never fails." However, it is also true that just as there are many new cures in the field of medicine, so in the field of church growth much more is known today than before about how churches grow.

McGAVRAN We do know more, yet as we study church growth around the world and improved ways of communicating the faith, we've discovered that generally faith is best communicated when there is fervent faith to communicate. When we believe that the most important thing a man can do is to get right with God, that there is no loss compared to eternal loss and no gain compared to eternal gain, then God abundantly blesses.

IN HOMES

ARN Back to "New Church"! I envision this church having many small meetings throughout the new community. Neighbors come into the homes of members for informal Bible study. On Sundays the congregation gathers in a rented hall, but during the week members' homes are used for small-group gatherings.

McGAVRAN These home meetings would be very much like New Testament churches, because the New Testament church, for perhaps 150 years, didn't build buildings. It met in homes. What you have said about the church consisting of many small, face-to-face-groups, open to the world, is exactly on target. If you look at growing congregations around the world, you'll find that most of them are strong in house-churches.

SHOULD WE BUILD?

ARN Yes, *but* as I inspect this profile I find "New Church" showing concern about a building.

*"A church scarcely gets organized before
it says, 'Now we really ought to have a building. . . .' "*

McGAVRAN I'm afraid you are right. A church scarcely gets organized before it says, "Now we really ought to have a building which is going to cost us $100,000 or $150,000." Christians get scared at the financial burden and all the problems that come with a new physical plant. Of course, a building is a good thing, but in balance. As I observe new churches that have been started and have grown, I see many which, for a year to ten years, have met in facilities not their own.

A new church is growing in Providence, Rhode Island. It meets in a big downtown hotel in the ballroom which is empty at eleven o'clock Sunday mornings. Adequate parking facilities, too, are available at that time. The church is growing rapidly, paying a small rent for a rather large facility. You'll find churches meeting in schools, barns, or dance halls. I worshiped quite a number of times in a church that met in a dance hall. The men assembled at nine o'clock in the morning and within half an hour had transformed the dance hall into a worshipful little church.

After church dismissed at 12:15, they used the next half hour turning it back into a gaudy dance hall. The physical plant, you see, is not the first need. It's just a nice convenience.

ARN In Wilmington, Delaware, where I planted a church, we used a bar restaurant on Sundays. It was an adequate place to meet, also very inexpensive. However, I always had to arrive an hour early to air it out. The smell of liquor and stale cigarettes was overpowering. With proper ventilation, however, it was a fine sanctuary and one God used to bring many to Himself.

McGAVRAN Back in the 1940's, I was home on furlough from India doing deputation work in Montana. I visited a beautiful church, just recently completed. Members said I should have seen the place where they met for twelve years—all through the depression—while they were getting started.

I asked, "Where was it?"

They replied, "In a room above the saloon. And twice while we were meeting there, while the church service was in progress, somebody fired a pistol up through the floor. Bang! Bang!"

I could not avoid wisecracking, "That must have kept you awake during the sermon."

Christians do start churches in all kinds of places, and *should*. That's the way Christians did in the New Testament."

GROWTH GOALS

ARN Should "New Church"—just beginning, vibrant, alive, only a few members—have growth goals?

McGAVRAN I think so—two kinds. First, growth goals

for the congregation. They ought to project how many members they hope to have, pray to have, this year, next year, and for each of the succeeding five years. These goals ought to be realistic in terms of the community. Know your community! Know where the new roads are, the new subdivisions, what kinds of people are coming in. With this information at their finger tips, members can make their evangelistic efforts count.

A friend of mine, formerly a missionary in the Philippines, now pastors a 115-member church in New Mexico. It has established growth goals for each of the coming five years.

That brings me to the second type of growth goals. This church in New Mexico is not only planning growth for itself, but is planning to start daughter churches—one in 1974, and two in 1975-76. By 1977 there will be a cluster of four churches, a mother church and three daughter churches, each prospering because of the presence of the others.

Church-growth goals for the mother church must not be selfish goals. They must not be, "We will start a church. We will bring people into ourselves." Rather they should be, "We will both bring people into ourselves and start new churches, nurturing them with love, affection, and cash on occasion, so that they may become strong, growing churches."

NEEDED: CLASS THREE LEADERS

ARN That's what I call "seeing the possibilities" right from the beginning. Did you hear that the members of "New Church" are looking for a part-time pastor?

McGAVRAN That is very good. At this stage a part-time pastor is all *they* need. If they were to have a full-time pastor now, they might become a clergy-dominated

133

church. A part-time pastor will allow some pastoral input and yet will correctly leave a great deal of the responsibility in the hands of the laymen of the church.

ARN If this church were subsidized and could afford it, would you recommend a full-time pastor?

McGAVRAN No! I don't think so. If the laymen are carrying their share of the load, there is great value in a "tent-making" ministry. Hundreds of small growing churches across the United States have part-time pastors. I've met pastors who earn their living pumping gas, teaching school, or working in a post office or a factory. If part-time pastors are backed up by laymen anxious to work, it is a wonderful combination. It means that new churches can be established at small cost. The Methodists did this when they were expanding. Some Baptists are doing this today. The Pentecostals are doing this all across Latin America. When one asks why Pentecostal churches are growing in Latin America, at least part of the answer is that most of their leaders are tent-making ministers. Incidentally, this pays off in another way. The minister himself becomes more a part of the community if he is earning his living in the rough-and-tumble of everyday life.

ARN Is he not looked down upon by the congregation and by others if he works in secular as well as "sacred" ways?

McGAVRAN I don't think he'll be looked down upon by the congregation. He may be by some ministers whose ecclesiastical tradition is such that none of their ministers work. Some static denominations are inclined to scorn tent-making ministers, but they should reflect on the fact that Paul himself was a tent-maker!

ARN Churches grow by using Class Three leaders. We need to underscore that.

A characteristic of a growing church is that it plans to develop leaders. "New Church" should have an effective program to develop leaders to supplement the tent-making pastor and to do many things he cannot do.

McGAVRAN When you ask, "Why do you have a tent-making pastor?", the church must not simply say, "All we can afford is a part-time minister; therefore, we are content to limp along." That's not the right answer. The right answer is a group of active, energetic laymen trained, as you suggest, in evangelistic techniques, meeting for prayer, seeking God's will, and *rejoicing in being an important part* of the ministry of the church.

A MODEL

ARN Christians who are obedient to the New Testament commission of going into all the world to preach the gospel and establish churches might find in "New Church" a model to be emulated by many individuals and many groups across the world.

McGAVRAN Across the world, yes, and across the United States. "New Church" is a prototype. We need thousands of "New Churches." Growing denominations here in the United States are planting many new churches. Church growth means, in part, growth into existing congregations, and in part, planting many small churches. Let us assume that 50 million people in the United States are unchurched . . .

ARN . . . and our goal is to reach them.

McGAVRAN How many "New Churches" would it

135

take at one hundred members a church to reach that 50 million?

ARN It would take . . . 500,000 new churches. Impossible!

McGAVRAN Since many of the 50 million would join existing churches, we would not need 500,000 new churches. But we *would* need and *must* have multitudes of new churches. We need multitudes of Christian fellowships—free, earnest, innovative, sensitive to the leading of the Holy Spirit—so that as the revival of Christianity comes upon us, we're ready. We cannot be stopped by believing that to get a church going we must have an investment of $100,000 to $200,000. That investment is wholly secondary. It's only a convenience. If a denomination has $100,000 or $200,000 and wants to spend it that way, that's fine. But we need multitudes of new churches which for maybe 5, 10, 15, 20 years are not bothered with a church building.

I was in a Western city last year and found a whole new "denomination" consisting of 25 house-churches meeting Sunday after Sunday. Each church numbered from 15 to 30 people—as many as could meet in a home. Wonderful Christians, living new lives and not bothered in the least about building church buildings!

ARN "New Church" is a prototype, a model of what could happen as Christians see the vision of a multitude of churches in the homogeneous groups in America and around the world.

McGAVRAN Once you get outside the United States, the number of new churches actually arising these days is legion. If Christ tarries for another fifty years, we shall see hundreds of thousands of new churches arising on this

136

globe. Church extension of this dimension is normal. We should praise God for it and for letting us be part of it.

CHAPTER 9

"*Changing Church*"

ARN Let's apply church-growth principles to a common type of church which I've called "Changing Church."

Its 50th anniversary was celebrated with speeches, dinners and remembrances. Yet the celebration had the aura of a funeral, for all sensed the future decline and death of the church if present trends continued.

The membership rolls carry approximately 400; however, Sunday morning attendance centers around the 200 mark. Two morning services are held, although they could easily be combined into one.

Some ten to fifteen years ago the growth which the church had earlier known plateaued and the last five to seven years have seen a steady decline. The Sunday School has also been declining and at a more rapid rate than the church.

With the decline in membership, giving has slackened, and commitments to missions, denomination and staff

*"The community, once upper
middle-class white, has changed color
. . . the church is on the dividing line."*

have been curtailed. The church has many older adults
and few young families. Leadership is tightly held by a few
families and rigid in its structure and demands. This has
been a proud church and holds to its pride tenaciously.
The former pastor left in discouragement, and the pulpit
committee is presently seeking for a man who will resolve
their problems.

The physical plant is well located on a main street. Its
architecture reveals its age; however, its rooms and sanctuary are more than adequate for the church's program.

The community, once upper middle-class white, has
changed color. Black and Spanish Americans comprise
approximately half the community and whites the other
half. The church is located on the dividing line. While
"Changing Church" carries on a variety of programs, most
of them turn inward with little significant contact with the
community.

"Changing Church" is representative of many thousands of churches across America.

McGAVRAN Yes, you could find some like it in most of the fifty states.

WORKING OUT YOUR ANSWER

ARN How successful could we be in applying church-growth principles to this situation?

McGAVRAN Church-growth principles should be, and can be, applied here! But they apply in different measure to different churches. We will find many variations on this theme. A church in New England, let us say, with a Portuguese, Roman Catholic population flooding into the community, is different from a church in Birmingham, Alabama, with Blacks flooding in. That, again, is different from a church in Washington or Oregon where some other ethnic minority or a lumber-camp community has moved into the neighborhood. There are many variations; there is no one solution. Nevertheless, I am confident that church-growth principles apply.

ARN And so, as we begin this chapter together, we understand, and we hope our readers understand, that a few short lines in a profile cannot capture the full dynamic, the interactions and interrelationships of any given church, nor can our answers be more than thought starters.

McGAVRAN Those thinking along with us will have many ideas of their own as to how to apply church-growth principles. I hope what we say here simply lights their fires. We're not proposing ideas that will work everywhere, but rather saying: consider these solutions to the degree that they fit your situation. I hope everyone who studies

*"Then one day the church closes
its doors and sells the building,
and that's the end of that particular congregation."*

this book and participates in the accompanying workbook will apply growth principles to his own church. The one thing everybody must do is to work out a solution that isn't a surrender. His solution should leave the church victorious; it should lead the church into growth. Anything else is no solution at all. It is simply saying the problem is insoluble, and we do not agree with that.

ARN Every church has growth possibilities if we but see them and apply them. Let's consider the profile of "Changing Church" and endeavor to apply some church-growth principles. "Changing Church" has a real growth problem. What do you suggest such a church might do?

A FIRST OPTION

McGAVRAN There are two options. First, it may remain Caucasian, limp along year after year, and expect to die in ten years.

142

ARN Certainly that option has been chosen by many churches. Almost without exception, such a decision spells surrender . . . and death.

McGAVRAN Yes, the members gradually move away to suburbs; the older members die. They are not replaced. A smaller and smaller number assemble, getting more and more discouraged. Then one day the church closes its doors and sells the building, and that's the end of that particular congregation. This policy does not apply church-growth principles, isn't interested in church growth, and one day the church wakes up to find itself dead! With the changing community *its* chances of life have suddenly ceased to exist.

A SECOND OPTION

ARN If the first is really not an option, what about the second? Remember this community is half Caucasian and half Black or Chicano. The church presently is on the dividing line, but all projections indicate that these groups will continue to make inroads into the Caucasian community.

McGAVRAN The second option open to "Changing Church" is to multiply Christian cells in both the Chicano and the Black communities. "Changing Church" will begin to get large numbers of Chicano and Black Christians. Perhaps we're talking about a Baptist, Methodist, Lutheran, or Presbyterian church. Let's agree we're talking about a Lutheran church. The goal should be to get 100 Chicano Lutheran families and 100 Black Lutheran families.

ARN Do you mean they would all be in the church at this time?

McGAVRAN Not necessarily. Let's assume, for the time being, that these 200 families don't worship in the church.

ARN You're talking about segregation?

McGAVRAN No, I don't think so. I am *for* integration, but not as the one and only solution. I see in "Changing Church" a few Black families and a few Chicano families who happen to like that kind of program. They've been welcomed by the Lutheran church. They are, in general, the more affluent members of their communities, and for various reasons they have become members of the existing Lutheran Church.

ARN And you see these families, then, as a key to reaching that part of the community?

McGAVRAN I am suggesting that part of the program of the existing church is to start Lutheran Christian cells among the Chicanos, and Lutheran Christian cells among the Blacks. So that you have both integration and a vivid, vital church in each of those incoming communities. The Lutheran Black cells and the Lutheran Chicano cells would be led by their own people. They would have Black ministers of about *their* degree of education. They would have Chicano ministers of about *their* degree of education and income. The Lutheranism which would bind these culture units together would be fairly elastic. The Lutheranism of the Blacks and Chicanos would not closely resemble the Lutheranism of the old German or Scandinavian immigrants who were settled in this part of the city.

ARN Then, gradually, as these Christian cells grew spiritually and numerically, they would play a more and more prominant role in the life of "Changing Church." If

144

this Lutheran church is to grow, it must reproduce Lutheran churches in the community. The place to begin is in small cell-groups.

McGAVRAN Yes, that Lutheran church must reproduce Christianity. In that changing community "Changing Church" cannot—repeat, cannot—reproduce affluent Caucasian-culture churches. You can put that down and sign it. The affluence isn't there, nor is the Caucasian culture there. But "Changing Church" can reproduce its earnest biblical Christianity. It can build churches of Blacks and Chicanos who have committed their lives absolutely to Jesus Christ.

On the mission fields around the world we call these indigenous churches. In India there are literally tens of thousands of Presbyterians whose average income is $60.00 a year—a year! They have little in common with Presbyterians in the United States who have an annual income of $16,000 a year. Yet they're all Presbyterians. Now, if that can happen in India, it can happen in the United States. We can have thoroughly Christian churches in two cultures, and each will fit its own culture.

FACING PROBLEMS

ARN That sounds fine in theory, but think of the problems.

McGAVRAN There will be problems, of course. For example, the unpaid or slightly paid voluntary leaders, the "pastors" of the house-churches and storefront churches will not have nearly as much education as the minister of the affluent Caucasian church.

ARN In fact, if they had much education, that in itself

would separate them from their Black and Chicano members and make them less effective.

McGAVRAN Remember that no matter how little education they have, they will have more than St. Peter had when he was planting churches throughout Judea!

ARN You're suggesting that a minister or lay leader who is a few steps ahead of his congregation can minister better than one a mile ahead?

McGAVRAN Very much better. And furthermore, I'm insisting that the educated ministers not draw too rigid a line between themselves and leaders of less education. Since they all love Jesus Christ, preach His word, and administer the sacraments, they are all "fellow ministers" together.

ARN Possibly a starting point would be with children and youth.

McGAVRAN This is a real possibility. You see, the youth are studying together, whereas the older generations seldom see each other. The boys and girls who are playing on the same basketball team, singing in the same high school choruses, and learning in the same high school classes, will find that they have a lot in common. These separate cell-groups in the different cultural communities would find many occasions to get together at "Changing Church" in a creative and brotherly fashion.

ARN As we're discussing problems, let's face a real one —money! Who's going to pay for these house-churches?

McGAVRAN The whole indigenous-church method and philosophy insists that churches in other cultures must be self-supporting, from the day they begin. Perhaps not absolutely so, but substantially so very early in their careers. We are not talking about a series of social-service projects for the poor people in our community, in which affluent Christians are doing something for poor people! There is no future in that. Sooner or later the affluent church folds and ceases to be, and when it does, its philanthropic program also ceases. That's just what we're *not* talking about.

If we establish indigenous churches, then right from the beginning they must be substantially self-supporting. They are self-supporting at their economic level and at the level of their vision. They are self-supporting in the same way that storefront churches are self-supporting. For example, New York City is a notoriously expensive place to live. Yet, among the New York Puerto Ricans, there are literally hundreds of storefront churches. Nobody subsidizes these. Groups of Puerto Rican Christians rent a store, carry on a church in it, and pay a part-time pastor *at their level*. The same thing could be done by any Christian cell provided it has a vigorous and vital Christian experience.

ARN You're saying that if a church wants to start other churches, the sooner it encourages them into self-support the healthier it is?

McGAVRAN It's my considered opinion that the greatest Christian treasure is not a play program for the youth. It's not more clothes or more food. It's not entertainment. If we really want to help people, we need to help them to become new creatures in Christ. Our Lord said, "Seek first the kingdom of God and His righteousness, and all these things shall be added unto you." (See Matt. 6:33.) And that is absolutely true. During the nineteenth century, you will remember, the Methodist church multiplied, not in the affluent sections of society, but in the poorer sections of society. As the poor became ardent Christians, the Lord abundantly blessed them. You won't find many poor Methodists today! The Lord does bless those who earnestly seek to follow Him.

A DEFINITE CHOICE

ARN Before any of these possibilities can be acted upon, "Changing Church" has to solve a bigger problem. Its members must see the possibilities. Now, seeing the growth possibilities for one's own cultural group is easy, but the leaders of "Changing Church" must look through Christ's eyes to the growth possibilities of other cultural groups.

Leaders must also recognize that the methods of "Evangelism Two" (evangelism in another culture) must be applied. If these two principles of church growth are applied to "Changing Church's" problem, there is hope.

So, "Changing Church" is at a point of decision. If it does nothing, it is going to die. If it applies church-growth principles, it has a good chance to live.

McGAVRAN Yes, a decision must be made, not ten or fifteen years down the road, at which time the church will disintegrate, but immediately. The church occupying that building will some day be Chicano or Black, but it will still be Lutheran, and "Changing Church" will not have lost its witness in that part of the city.

ARN Have you ever seen this happen in "real life"?

McGAVRAN I'm thinking just now of an affluent Caucasian church on the edge of Watts in Los Angeles. Ten years ago, it had the opportunity of engaging in a vigorous program of evangelism in the Black community. It turned down that opportunity. While it admitted a few Blacks, the more affluent and the better educated, it remained out of touch with the main Black community. Then, when the crunch came, when the moment of truth occurred, it had to sell its half million dollar building to a completely different denomination. The old Caucasian church folded, broke up, and there is no church of that denomination there anymore. Had it applied church-growth principles ten years ago, it would by this time have had 200 or 300 families of its persuasion in that part of town.

ARN   A decision to turn over a church to people of another culture and background is a very difficult decision for Caucasian Americans, especially when the church has been a proud one.

McGAVRAN   Yes, this is true. It *is* a difficult decision.

ARN   But difficult as it may seem, the Christian faith must be transmitted regardless of culture barriers.

McGAVRAN   We cannot bring, and don't want to bring, everyone into our culture. They have their cultures, rich and beautiful, and the Christian faith ought to be growing in all cultures.

ARN   The Christian faith is like a vine which can grow on many different trellises. Too often the trellis and the vine have been thought of as one and the same.

A THIRD OPTION

ARN   I believe there is a third option for "Changing Church"—that the congregation move to a new community. That might solve many problems.

McGAVRAN   If this church which we are calling Lutheran, decides to pull out, it will sell the building to people with whom it has very little in common. That's possible, of course, but is not a good solution. It is far better for "Changing Church," while it is still vigorous and has life and power, with the Holy Spirit dwelling in its members, to communicate its faith to the people around its doors who don't know Jesus Christ . . .

ARN So ten years from now, those new Christians will have taken over the church, and the Caucasians will have joined churches or started churches in the communities to which they have moved.

McGAVRAN That would be a satisfying solution, wouldn't it?

APPLYING GROWTH CHARACTERISTICS

ARN Let's apply some characteristics of growing churches to "Changing Church." For example, growing churches have growth goals.

McGAVRAN Yes, the members of this church have been carrying on year after year with only vague, if any, growth goals. In place of that, they need to establish sensible growth goals which apply to the real mixed racial community of which they are now a part.

ARN Another characteristic of growing churches is that they plan to develop leaders.

McGAVRAN Exactly! Here again, that old Caucasian church simply said, "We have leaders. We know what deacons and elders in this church look like. We know what session members look like. We know how they should talk, how they should dress, where they should live. We

150

have standards, and we choose leaders who come up to those standards." That was fine in the homogeneous Caucasian community thirty years ago. But that community no longer exists. The leadership standards must fit the real situation. Black leaders will not have the same degree of education the old Caucasians had. They'll be just as Christian but will have less education. Furthermore, these 100 Black families and the 100 Chicano families will not be won if their only leaders are Caucasians. Of the 100 Black families, a good percentage must be Black leaders, chosen from among the Blacks—Black preachers, Black deacons, and Black elders! These new Christian cells (Black and Chicano) must be self-respecting, self-governing, self-propagating and self-supporting. That's the only way they'll multiply and the only way they'll function.

ARN In the development of leadership, "Changing Church" must start training men out of the homogeneous groups in which the Faith is growing.

McGAVRAN We already do that, you know, in regard to youth. Youth is a distinct sub-culture, and we go out of our way to make sure that the youth in our churches are led by other youth. We don't put gray-haired men and gray-haired women in charge of the young people in any church. We get youth leaders.

ARN "Changing Church" is seeking a new pastor. If I were on the pulpit committee, I would look for a bold man, who knows how to plant churches in changing communities, who sees the broader possibilities, and who trains laymen out of new groups becoming Christians.

In any event, "Changing Church" has many fine Christians who can wrestle with the problems and, with God's help, emerge victorious.

151

CHAPTER 10

"Suburban Church"

ARN The profile of this church indicates growth, health and vitality. The people of "Suburban Church" are comfortable and happy. Their membership represents a cross section of the community, with young families being the most numerous.

Many of the members commute to their employment in a nearby city. While the community has stability, there is a large turnover of families every year as men are transferred to other job locations.

Sunday sees the church well filled at both services. The Sunday School has continued to grow and expand. The church strongly emphasizes Christian nurture.

"Suburban Church" has facilities which have been built in recent years. While not new, they are contemporary and fit the economic level of the community. One problem the Board struggles with is not enough classroom space to meet the growth needs. Offerings and gifts have been adequate to meet operating needs, but economic pressure on the many young families has limited giving to the church.

"Suburban Church" is well located in relationship to the community. Once a small town a few miles from the city, this community has grown tremendously during the last decade. New homes have been constructed; schools and small businesses have flourished. In the midst of this receptive segment of the population, "Suburban Church" has grown and appears vital.

McGAVRAN A good description! And there are thousands of such churches in the United States. The opportunity for "Suburban Church" to multiply is tremendous, if for no other reason than that numbers of suburban areas will continue to increase.

ARN Churches such as this are a major strength of American Protestantism.

SEEING THE POSSIBILITIES

McGAVRAN They will grow even stronger in the future. Great megalopolises will develop from Chicago to Pittsburgh, from Boston to Washington, from San Francisco to San Diego. As urbanized areas grow, there will be literally tens of thousands of opportunities for churches as you have described.

ARN I wonder if Christians will see the opportunity?

McGAVRAN They must! The responsible leaders of the churches must understand that God has placed them in a very favorable situation and given them an unparalleled opportunity for growth.

ARN Unfortunately, the magnitude of the opportunity is frequently not realized.

"I wonder if Christians will see the opportunity?"
"They must!"

McGAVRAN One reason is that "Suburban Church" thinks small. Since the congregation has experienced some growth, they relax, reasoning that they are doing fairly well. Something much more is needed.

ESTABLISHING GROWTH GOALS

ARN One thing is that "Suburban Church" needs to establish growth goals.

McGAVRAN Exactly!

ARN We have discussed how charts and graphs help reveal the previous patterns of church growth, but now comes the important step of projecting goals to the future.

McGAVRAN This projection is a step of faith and must be seen as such.

ARN Certainly tomorrow's goals should not be built on yesterday's mistakes. Again and again, I have observed budget committees look at last year's budget as the major guide for the new budget. That approach will only compound the problems and limit the possibilities of growth. Expanded vision is demanded.

McGAVRAN It's a matter of seeing the possibilities and knowing you are God's instrument to achieve them.

ARN Faith goals must be big, big enough to include God's plan. If goals are projected, which we know can be reached by our own strength, our own efforts, where is faith? Where is God?

McGAVRAN An excellent example of what can happen when faith goals are established was given to me by Dr. Charles Chaney of Springfield, Illinois. He told me how the Southern Baptists have in recent years planted over 400 churches in that state! This church planting took place, mind you, while many churches and denominations in Illinois were standing around wringing their hands at "the irrelevant church in the post-Christian era," bemoaning the indifferent population and wondering whether the church had any future!

Goal-setting produces results. The Southern Baptists, according to Dr. Chaney, are planning to plant 600 more churches in Illinois in the next thirty years. That is the sort of sensible, aggressive growth-thinking that so many more can do.

ARN Goal-setting is effective not only at the denominational level, but also at the local church level; in fact, the more larger goals are broken down into smaller parts, the more effective they become, and the more involvement you have in the goal-setting process.

McGAVRAN What do you mean?

ARN Goals to be effective must be "owned" by all involved. For example, a pastor who tells his congregation, "Our goal for the next year is 400 house calls, 100 new families in the Sunday School, and 150 new church members" is establishing goals, but they are *his* goals, not necessarily those of the congregation. Unfortunately, what often happens in such a situation is the congregation will give verbal agreement to the goals, but will not involve themselves in their accomplishment. Why should they? They have not bought them. They do not "own" them.

As the weeks progress and the goals become more elusive, the pastor tends to "whip" the congregation into action. However, this "whipping" only brings alienation and tension, and soon the pastor is convinced he should leave for a more fruitful field.

There is a better way!

Goals must be "owned" and this "owning" takes place as the members share in establishing these goals. In the case of "Suburban Church," the pastor should first establish a "climate" for growth, a climate created by helping his people see the reasons for, and opportunities of, growth. A next step would be to invite the various groups of the church to participate in a growth effort. After discussion and prayer each group would establish its faith-growth goals. The accumulated goals would represent the overall church-growth goals for that period. Recognition, encouragement, and progress reports would be an important part of the effort.

As the weeks progress, people would be working toward the accomplishing of the goals because the goals are theirs. They "own" them because they had a part in their establishment. The church grows, the people are happy as they see "their results," and the pastor feels God has called him to many years of rich harvest and service.

"These individualistic efforts
pull the church in many
different directions, making
overall progress difficult,
if not impossible."

"When energies ... are
harnessed by unifying goals
... the church moves forward."

McGAVRAN   Oh, I agree that everybody works harder at goals they had a part in shaping.

ARN   There is another truth we must recognize. If a church is to progress toward a goal, it must harness the available energy and focus that energy on the goal to be achieved.

In churches where goals are not clearly defined, you will usually find individual groups or organizations doing their own "thing." These individualistic efforts pull the church in many different directions, making overall progress difficult, if not impossible.

However, when the energies of the individual groups and organizations are harnessed by unifying goals, there is a concentration of effort which makes progress possible. The available energy, rather than being dissipated, is channeled and the church moves forward.

McGAVRAN   There's a psychological problem, namely fear of failure, connected with goal setting.

ARN   True! If you have no goals, you need not fear failure. Fear frustrates faith. I'm convinced that freedom to fail is a most important freedom and one that pastor and people must recognize as inherent in any significant effort.

Imagine that "Suburban Church" established a goal of 150 new convert-members in the next year. At the conclusion of that effort they had reached 100. Is that failure? Of course not; it's success! In all probability, it's 100 more than would have been reached without a goal.

Goals may be revised. Let us say, "Suburban Church" established a goal but later discovered that circumstances changed, and the goal was no longer valid. It should change it to a realistic faith-goal.

McGAVRAN   We agree that "Suburban Church," and

160

any church, should say to itself, "We have a responsibility to establish church-growth goals in keeping with the opportunities that God has set before us."

SMALL-GROUP INVOLVEMENT

ARN Let's continue. A characteristic of a growing church is that it utilizes small groups.

McGAVRAN Many rapidly growing churches soon lose their personal touch. As people move into and out of a community, in this mobile American population, they don't form close associations and the church becomes a rather impersonal place. You may greet people and be greeted, but the intimate, close, friendly relationship which human beings need so much is not there.

ARN The need for relationships is best met in small Christian groups. Members of such groups come to know others at significantly deeper levels than in "regular" church activities. They share a Christian love, concern and understanding for others in the group. They feel a freedom to be honest, to remove the masks, to be themselves. They know the deeper meanings of "brother" or "sister" in the Lord.

McGAVRAN Small groups are greatly needed and are being greatly blessed across America. "Suburban Church" could find in them a touch of the early church, as well as helpful and rewarding relationships which penetrate the entire congregation.

ARN It's accurate to say, I believe, that the larger the church and the more rapid its growth, the more essential is a small-group ministry.

McGAVRAN   And probably the more fruitful. Added to the advantages and benefits of small groups, are the advantages of the large church. So if the large church has many small vital groups, you have the best of both, the advantages of bigness and the intimacy of smallness.

OUTREACH

ARN   With a growing church such as we are considering, does the need for direct outreach diminish?

McGAVRAN   The great temptation of "Suburban Church" is to count on its favorable location to do the job.

ARN   And this isn't sufficient?

McGAVRAN   It is not! "We're well located. We have a five-acre plot on a prominent street. Everybody knows us." "We've engaged the services of a fine minister." "The best people in town come and worship with us." "We have a fine kindergarten." "Our choir is the best in town." These are all plus-factors which make it easy to join such a church. But if that's all there is, then Christianity becomes superficial. Direct evangelism is an essential part of such a church. Church-growth principles say, "Don't depend on external advantages." Church-growth principles say, "Engage in direct evangelism, confronting people with the commands of Christ." People must know that the great treasure of the Christian faith is something entirely divorced from these external advantages.

LEADERSHIP DEVELOPMENT

ARN   A church such as "Suburban" should give special attention to the deployment of its leadership. We previously discussed various types of leadership in a church

162

and certainly this church should employ a strategy which deploys leadership in both maintenance and outreach ministry.

McGAVRAN The temptation of the affluent church is to be concerned with itself. Even if it does some good work in missions overseas or in philanthropic programs in the inner city, it tends to be satisfied with itself. But if it really wants spiritual health, a large proportion of its members must be talking to other people about Jesus Christ. They are giving witness as to what He means to them. They are praying for other people. They are speaking about a new quality of life that men cannot have unless they become His disciples and followers of The Way.

ARN "Suburban Church" needs to study carefully the deployment of its people in ministry. It needs to discover the number of its Class One and Class Two leaders and then take appropriate steps to assure proper balance.

EVANGELISM—EDUCATION

ARN Let's come to grips with another issue which faces all churches but which has special implications for a church such as we are discussing. At "Suburban Church" the attitude is this: "We are growing. The big need is for perfecting. The church is called to teach Christians to live in the world as Christians. If this is accomplished, evangelism, mission, stewardship, will all find their proper places." In other words, what "Suburban Church" members are saying is, "We feel a tension between evangelism and education."

McGAVRAN It is a mistake to emphasize that "tension." It is not either evangelism or Christian education, it is rather *both* evangelism *and* Christian education. If

163

Christian education, for example, is unconcerned about whether neighbors, friends, relatives come to know Jesus Christ, it is not Christian. In order to be really Christian, education must throb with the passion that other people know Jesus Christ.

ARN And evangelism too must have concern for growth in grace. Evangelism is incomplete if it rushes from "soul" to "soul," unconcerned whether the new convert grows, matures, and reproduces. Adequate evangelism, for me, must be concerned with the whole person. As you said, it is neither evangelism nor Christian education. It is *both* combined in a united effort to carry out the Scripture, "Go into all the world and teach." It is not "go" by itself or "teach" by itself. The two are inseparably interrelated.

McGAVRAN If one analyzes that particular passage, he sees that the command is to "make disciples." How do you make them? You make them by *going* and by *teaching.* Making disciples is the command, and going and teaching are the methods by which Christians carry out the orders. "Suburban Church" needs to do both.

ARN One problem, however, is that for "Suburban Church" Christian education is always easier than evangelism. Christian education is serving ourselves, our children, youth and adults.

McGAVRAN Yes, evangelism is more difficult. Evangelism is essentially doing things for other people which may be interpreted as being unduly concerned about their welfare, and impertinent. Because of that, many Christians in Suburbia are inclined not to do much in the way of evangelism. Often a church is heavy on Christian education, light on evangelism, and doesn't begin to develop its real capacities for evangelism.

ARN I think history illustrates two things: One is that Christianity cannot exist without Christian education, and two, that when the church has flourished, it has created its own distinctive kind of education. For example, in America the Sunday School has played a significant role in church development.

McGAVRAN Yes, it has, and there's a good deal of evidence that churches grow as the church school flourishes. However, when the evidence is examined carefully, you find that the relationship is not automatic. It's not that *if* you have a Sunday School, the church will grow. It is rather that if you have a Sunday School of a certain sort, the church will grow. So that here again, one needs to look— every church needs to look—at its own Sunday School very carefully. Is it responsible for a 4, 5, or 6 percent per annum growth in the church? If it isn't, then we must not comfort ourselves, saying, "Well, we've got a good Sunday School. If we just make it a little better, the church will grow."

ARN Let's expand that idea to all organizations in the church. In other words, all groups should play substantial parts in a growing church.

McGAVRAN That's why it is so very important that all the organizations of the church see themselves in a double light. For example, the men's group makes for good fellowship. The men get together, have a good time, come to know each other, and study the Bible. But the men's organization must not stop there. The men's organization, if properly understood, is also a means for reaching other men. Now, it's at the outreach point that many churches in America are weak. It is easier to serve one's self than it is to serve other people.

ARN I have smiled inwardly as I've seen men's groups get together for what they say is fellowship. They'll sit around, they'll eat, they'll throw darts, they'll listen to a speaker. However, they yawn and are bored; meaningful fellowship is rather thin. An energized group of men is busy putting on a church roof, doing neighborhood visitation, or serving Christ with a purpose. Fellowship follows as a by-product of a greater purpose. A group with motive for ministry would contribute to the growth of "Suburban Church."

McGAVRAN One of the closest fellowships I ever saw in a church was in a men's group determined that it was going to reach its town for Christ. The members undertook a survey to determine need and then presented the gospel in many different ways of evangelism. In weekly meetings they reported on what had been done and then they planned and prayed for the future. In this meaningful work they had much good fellowship and came to know each other very intimately.

EVANGELISM—SOCIAL ACTION

ARN Another possible tension in "Suburban Church" is that which can exist between evangelism and social action. For example, I have heard such statements as, "How can a church talk of evangelism when the world in which we live has so many problems: hunger, poverty, prejudice, hatred? And you as a church are interested in evangelism? Your words of evangelism have little meaning if you're not involved in the *real issues of today's world.*"

McGAVRAN Yes, we've both heard the argument. People say that unless we solve these problems, we don't have a credible witness. I have difficulty with that argument. It overlooks the meaningful Christian witness in our country, perhaps particularly in suburbia. I grant you there are problems in North America—poverty, prejudice, hatred—but we get nowhere by overstating the matter.

Actually the Christian witness in North America is rather dynamic. The tremendous amount of good will Christians pour out, the free time they give to community projects, the civic enterprises they carry on!! Here in America the church has put a moral and ethical foundation under all of life, which has to be seen to be believed. You've got to live out of the country for 30 years, as I did, to come back and see the difference.

ARN You're saying "Suburban Church" already has a credible witness, so let it be about evangelism?

McGAVRAN Yes, indeed! However, nothing I have said should give anyone the impression that we're perfect. There is still a great deal to do and injustices to be straightened out, but most suburban churches have plenty of Christian goodness to give credibility to any amount of evangelism they may do. Furthermore, we must never forget that in evangelism we're not telling people how good we are. We preach Christ, not ourselves. If we start preaching ourselves, we're done for; I don't care how good we are. We preach Christ, and what we're telling people is, "We also are sinners, but man, we have found a Saviour and we want you to find Him, too." That's essentially what evangelism is.

Let "Suburban Church" continue social action but not make the capital mistake of saying, "We can't do any evangelism until we do a lot more social action." "Suburban Church," to have the greatest joy in Christian life, should be passing on Christ. It must do more evangelism.

CHAPTER 11

Go and Grow

AUTOMATIC GROWTH?

ARN We've come a long way in our discussions on church growth, but I wonder if some of our readers might be saying something like this: "To carry on the whole program of God in the world is the mission of the church. While winning men to Christian faith is undoubtedly part of the program, it is by no means the foremost part."

McGAVRAN And they will argue that what each congregation, lay leader, and minister must do is to carry on the whole program of the church—teach in the Sunday School, maintain the building, preach good sermons, and carry on good organizations. From all of this, the church will grow automatically.

ARN But the automatic growth may not take place.

McGAVRAN All the evidence we have is that automatic growth doesn't take place. The greatest obstacle to the growth of the church is the belief in "splendid church work, whether the church grows or not." When we are

"Without clear-cut, aggressive plans for the growth of the church, there will be no growth."

engaged merely in splendid church work, the church does not grow. Without clear-cut, aggressive plans for the growth of the church, there will be no growth.

The church doesn't grow by carrying on good youth meetings, a good Sunday School, good preaching or a good choir unless these are inspired by a desire to see persons become disciples of Jesus Christ and responsible members of His church. If this is their dominant passion, then the organizations and programs will, of course, help the church to grow.

ARN But the answer comes back: "If we increase our activities and programs, if we intensify what we are doing and work harder at it, we'll grow."

McGAVRAN That is definitely not true. The assumption behind that thought is, "Of course, we're interested in church growth." But we've got to make a distinction between being interested in church growth in a vague sort of

170

way and being interested in church growth enough to know when we're growing and when we are not growing. We cannot just go on with endless activity, trusting that somehow or other the church will grow. There must be *plans* for a church to grow.

PLANNING FOR GROWTH

ARN Let's be more specific. Are there plans in the Scripture for church growth?

McGAVRAN Observe Paul planting churches; he had a very definite plan. He always spoke in the synagogue. His first message was that the Messiah had come. When a group of Jews by birth believed on Jesus as the Messiah, he then branched out to take in the proselytes and devout persons. From then on he spoke to the Gentiles. And when he was thrown out of a community, as he frequently was, he would go on to the next. Paul repeated that process again and again. Yes, Paul had a definite plan for church planting. He found what worked for him, and he kept on repeating it.

ARN When the church grows, whether in New Testament days or today, it grows because definite plans . . . bold plans . . . concrete plans . . . exciting plans . . . were made and carried out.

McGAVRAN We need definite plans proposed to the church board, debated, modified, accepted and put into effect, just as plans for a new building or for any new major church enterprise are formulated and put through the mill and into practice. Christians concerned with church growth must find ways to communicate Christ which actually increase the number of Christians, which actually multiply congregations, which actually work.

"When the church grows . . . it grows because definite plans . . . bold plans . . . concrete plans . . . exciting plans . . . were made and carried out."

ARN We're talking about formulating plans which have three parts: one, growth in the local congregation; two, planting new churches in America; and three, multiplying new churches in other countries. An individual church should be doing all three.

McGAVRAN Every church should be working in all these ways. Of course, its first responsibility is Jerusalem. Christians must see to it that the people of their own community are churched. It is not sufficient for a congregation to congratulate itself on being a church of 300 or 400 members. It must also be praying for the 3,000 or 4,000 people living in the general area who are living apart from Christ. Every church begins at Jerusalem.

Then it also has a responsibility as a part of the denomination. It would be very interesting, as we have said earlier, to chart the growth rate of the denomination. Members should see if their denomination is keeping up with the growth of the population, falling behind, or soaring ahead.

172

To make such a study would lead to making plans for denominational growth. This always involves planting new churches.

ARN And what of multiplying churches in other lands?

McGAVRAN Christians should be engaged in doing this. Two billion people are not Christians. Most of them have never even heard the name of Christ. There are so many opportunities for evangelism and church planting that every congregation and every denomination should aim at multiplying churches both here and across the seas. The church is the basic hope of the world. As people come to be Christians, as they allow Christ to have His way in their lives, as they pattern their lives upon the holy Scriptures, they will develop a quality of life which is greatly needed in the world today.

ARN So as churches formulate their plans for church growth, they must indeed turn to Scripture and hear: "Jerusalem, Judea, Samaria, and the uttermost parts of the earth."

McGAVRAN Yes, but not as a means of self-aggrandizement. Christians are not trying to conquer the world. We're trying to bless the world—to make this world the kind of place that God intends it to be, to give people, through Christ, the power to be loving, good, just and peaceful.

MODIFYING PLANS

ARN As a church puts growth plans into action, it will be necessary from time to time to make modifications.

McGAVRAN For one thing, conditions change, so

plans have to change. Some plans don't work well and consequently must be modified. Or perhaps plans work *so* well and transform the context so much that new plans are needed. Aggressive, intelligent and adequate plans must be flexible. We must modify them in the light of the feedback.

ATTEMPT GREAT THINGS FOR GOD

ARN   Let's discuss how big plans should be.

McGAVRAN   They should be adequate to the situation. If God has given us a great field or a great church, we will naturally make greater plans than if He has given us a small field or a small church. A large church in California is facing two million Spanish Americans, an enormous field. It is not sufficient for that large church to plan to gather in a small congregation of 40 or 50 Spanish Americans who happen to live in the vicinity. Plans must be adequate to the need. Bold plans! A great Spanish-American community is growing up. It will be a much better community if a reasonable number of its members, say a million, find new life in Christ. Churches in California, if they are to plan adequately, must think of churching all great unchurched populations. Our plans must be as great as human need and as encompassing as the purpose of God.

ARN   In formulating plans, we must ask ourselves what God's will is as He sends us out to minister to His lost sons and daughters.

FLOW CHART FOR GROWTH

ARN   To help organize and carry out plans for church growth, we can learn from the secular fields around us.

McGAVRAN   Indeed! Modern industry uses a sophisticated and intelligent form of planning that it calls a "pert" chart. In education it's called a "flow" chart. When one makes such a chart, he determines the goal to be achieved and sets this as his "terminal objective." For example, suppose we were going to build a church building. The goal to be achieved is a building of certain sizes and dimensions built on such and such a lot. That's the terminal objective. In a flow chart we set down all the steps necessary to reach our goal. These are called "enabling objectives." Such steps are: the decision by the church to build . . . purchasing property . . . estimating what the church can raise . . .

ARN . . . hiring an architect . . . approving plans . . . raising money . . . are additional steps.

McGAVRAN All these and other steps are then put on the chart in an appropriate sequence. When the pert chart is completed, you can see every step necessary to build a church building. It is then easy to work systematically at these enabling objectives and thus realize the long-range goal, the terminal objective.

ARN A similar chart can be easily designed for church growth.

McGAVRAN Suppose the goal of a church is to increase its membership from its present 340 to 800. The goal is a church of 800. The various steps necessary to reach that goal could then be charted. Or suppose that the goal was to unite with the other churches of this denomination to plant fifty new churches in this state. That would be the terminal objective on the flow chart. Various appropriate enabling objectives would have to be fitted in. The statement of purpose, the raising of finances, the training of men, the securing of properties, the creation of theolog-

GOAL: CHURCH GROWTH

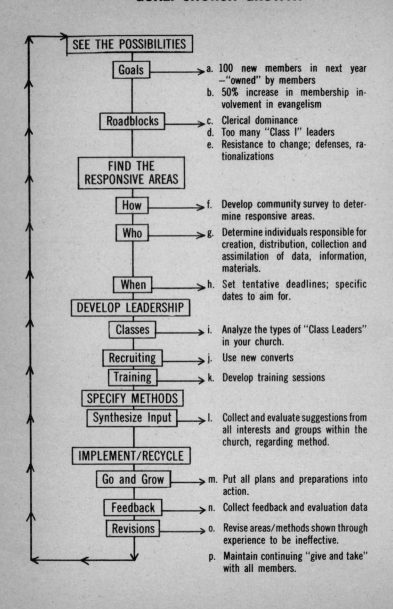

SEE THE POSSIBILITIES

Goals
- a. 100 new members in next year —"owned" by members
- b. 50% increase in membership involvement in evangelism

Roadblocks
- c. Clerical dominance
- d. Too many "Class I" leaders
- e. Resistance to change; defenses, rationalizations

FIND THE RESPONSIVE AREAS

How
- f. Develop community survey to determine responsive areas.

Who
- g. Determine individuals responsible for creation, distribution, collection and assimilation of data, information, materials.

When
- h. Set tentative deadlines; specific dates to aim for.

DEVELOP LEADERSHIP

Classes
- i. Analyze the types of "Class Leaders" in your church.

Recruiting
- j. Use new converts

Training
- k. Develop training sessions

SPECIFY METHODS

Synthesize Input
- l. Collect and evaluate suggestions from all interests and groups within the church, regarding method.

IMPLEMENT/RECYCLE

Go and Grow
- m. Put all plans and preparations into action.

Feedback
- n. Collect feedback and evaluation data

Revisions
- o. Revise areas/methods shown through experience to be ineffective.
- p. Maintain continuing "give and take" with all members.

ical conviction, the actual doing of the work—all of these, step by step, would come in the order of sequence.

"GIVE ME A MAN TO STAND IN THE GAP"

ARN Certainly such a chart would give us a logical plan and time sequence. However, for the plan to work, one element—personal commitment—is still missing. For success, God requires the individual, the layman or the pastor to say, "I am only one, but with God's help I commit myself to this task of winning men and of church growth."

McGAVRAN That's right. There must be individual responsibility. What is everyone's task is nobody's task. All of this discussion of church growth will do little good, unless and until, some of the individuals who are discussing the growth of the church will say, "I'm going to *do* something about this." Ideas must be clothed in flesh. A wonderful way to begin is prayer. If in any congregation a group were to pray and continue steadfastly in prayer that the church would grow, their church would grow.

ARN The Word invites us to pray that the Lord of the harvest might send forth laborers.

McGAVRAN Most churches need a great increase of Class Two workers—men and women who give time, who are individually responsible, who say, "The growth of the church is *my* business, and I'm going to do something about it."

ARN In conclusion, then, it all must start with personal commitment. Individual Christians must resolve with God's help to bring about church growth in their neighborhoods, suburbs and cities. This commitment turns growth plans into flesh and blood.

177

Additional Resources

BOOKS

McGavran, Donald. *Understanding Church Growth.* Grand Rapids: Eerdmans, 1970.

McGavran, Donald, ed. *Church Growth Bulletin.* South Pasadena: William Carey Library, 1969.

McGavran, Donald. *The Bridges of God.* New York: Friendship Press, 1955.

McGavran, Donald, ed. *Church Growth and Christian Mission.* New York: Harper & Row, 1965.

McGavran, Donald, ed. *Eye of the Storm, the Great Debate in Mission.* Waco: Word Books, 1972.

Tippett, Alan R. *Church Growth and the Word of God.* Grand Rapids: Eerdmans, 1970.

Wagner, C. Peter. *Frontiers in Missionary Strategy.* Chicago: Moody, 1971.

Winter, Ralph D. *The Twenty-Five Unbelievable Years.* South Pasadena: William Carey Library, 1969.

FILMS

Building the Church: This new series of films has been developed as a tool to help examine the basic strategy Paul employed in building the early church. Each of the six, color 16mm films in the series is approximately five minutes in length and will stimulate discussion or other interaction in preaching-teaching and with small groups. The series, photographed on location, is effectively used to study the growth of the early church and its implication for today. There is an Action Guide available for use with the series. Films in the series include:

"The Apostle Paul"
"Paul in Philippi"
"Paul in Thessalonica"
"Paul in Corinth"
"Paul in Ephesus"
"Paul in Rome"

Exploring the Churches of The Revelation: A series of eight five-minute color 16mm films which provides the historic, geographical, cultural setting of the churches of The Revelation. The series is excellent for studying these churches and for discovering the reasons for growth or no growth. Films in the series include:

"Patmos"
"Ephesus"
"Smyrna"
"Pergamum"
"Thyatira"
"Sardis"
"Philadelphia"
"Laodicea"

Both series available through Christian Communication, 1857 Highland Oaks Dr., Arcadia, California, 91006.

SEE THE FILM

HOW TO GROW A CHURCH is an excellent film for pastor and people who desire growth for their church — large, medium, small. It leads to the discovery of new growth possibilities and provides motivation for the growth.

Color / 28 Minutes / Rental $25.00

Order from the

**GOSPEL FILMS DISTRIBUTOR
NEAREST YOU**

or from

GOSPEL FILMS, INC.

P. O. Box 455 / Muskegon, Michigan 49443